Praise for *Write Where Yo*

"This practical but eloquent book sparkles ~~pii~~ors,
writing samples from young writers, and wonderful quotes from
writers such as Dr. Seuss, Jamaica Kincaid, Annie Dillard, and
May Sarton. Mirriam-Goldberg offers great references to the
world of writing and reading and even offers examples of music
from around the world that may inspire reflection and writing.
To many a young writer, this book will be as delicious and
nourishing as homemade bread with fresh strawberry jam.
I am giving it to my daughter."

MARY PIPHER, PH.D., AUTHOR OF REVIVING OPHELIA: SAVING THE SELVES
OF ADOLESCENT GIRLS

3/00

"This book should help young people hitch their creativity to
the stars of their needs and their ambitions. I wish I had had a
book like this when I was a teen."

JAMES GUNN, AUTHOR OF THE IMMORTALS AND EDITOR OF
THE ROAD TO SCIENCE FICTION SERIES

WRITE

WHERE YOU ARE

How to Use Writing
to Make Sense of Your Life

A GUIDE FOR TEENS

by Caryn Mirriam-Goldberg, Ph.D.

Edited by Elizabeth Verdick & Darsi Dreyer

free spirit
PUBLISHING
Works
for kids®

Library of Congress Cataloging-in-Publication Data

Mirriam-Goldberg, Caryn.
     Write where you are : how to use writing to make sense of your life: a guide for teens / by Caryn Mirriam-Goldberg.
          p.   cm.
     Includes bibliographical references and index.
     Summary: Provides advice and exercises to enable individuals to become more confident and more competent writers.
     ISBN 1-57542-060-0
     1. Creative writing—Problems, exercises, etc.—Juvenile literature. 2. Self-perception in adolescence—Juvenile literature. 3. Diaries—Authorship—Juvenile literature. 4. Creative writing—Juvenile literature.
     [1. Creative writing. 2. Authorship.] I. Title.
     LB1631.M459   1999
     808.042'0712—dc21   98-54292
                                                                                      CIP
                                                                                      AC

Excerpt from "The Weight of Sweetness" copyright © 1986 by Li-Young Lee. Reprinted from *Rose,* poems by Li-Young Lee, with the permission of BOA Editions, Ltd.

Cover design and typesetting by Percolator
Text Illustrations by Dao Nguyen
Index compiled by Randl Ockey

The following are registered trademarks of Free Spirit Publishing Inc.:
FREE SPIRIT®
FREE SPIRIT PUBLISHING®
SELF-HELP FOR TEENS®
SELF-HELP FOR KIDS®
WORKS FOR KIDS®
THE FREE SPIRITED CLASSROOM®

free spirit PUBLiSHiNG®   Works for kids®

10 9 8 7 6 5 4 3 2 1
Printed in the United States of America

Free Spirit Publishing Inc.
400 First Avenue North, Suite 616
Minneapolis, MN 55401-1724
(612) 338-2068
help4kids@freespirit.com
www.freespirit.com

*In gratitude for all my teachers and
especially for Judith Rance-Roney, Alan C. Kough,
and Phil Brater, wherever you are.*

Acknowledgments

Thank you to all who contributed their writing, thinking, and insights to this book, especially the teens in the "Me, Myself, I" writing workshop at Topeka Collegiate School who actively shared themselves and their words. I am also very grateful to all the school administrators and teachers who made it possible for me to visit many senior and junior high schools throughout Kansas during the last decade. Thanks to Free Spirit for believing in this project. Most of all, perpetual bouquets to my editor, Elizabeth Verdick, who worked with me to grow a little book into a big dream.

Contents

Part 3: Surfacing:
The Vision of Revision

Introduction

I was fourteen when I sat on the concrete steps in front of my soon-to-be ex-best friend's apartment after a major fight. This screaming match would end the first and—up until that point—only real friendship of my life. At home, both of my parents, in the middle of the century's worst divorce (so I thought), had barricaded themselves into separate halves of the house, and I wasn't sure which side I belonged on. I thought my life was ruined, and I didn't know what to do.

So I started writing.

How Writing Saved My Life

My first poem, not surprisingly, was about how cruel people could be. So was the second. And the third. But in the process of holding a pen and guiding it back and forth over each line, I began to feel a sense of hope. I started to feel a little less scared, a little less alone. I liked this feeling, so I kept writing.

For the past twenty-five years, I've kept writing—sometimes fast and sloppy, other times as slow as traffic jams. Today I have shelves full of journals, and drawers full of poems, essays, stories, and letters. Writing has become the center of my life, beating through all I know about myself and the world like the heart beats through the body, bringing me back again and again to the blankness of the page and the need to fill it. Writing has saved my life.

I believe writing down my thoughts, poems, and stories— sometimes for hours each day—kept me from thinking too much about suicide during a difficult and desperate time. As a teen, I wondered if I truly deserved to live, and writing helped me make sense of my pain. When I wrote, I could gather on the page my fear and other overwhelming emotions, creating a kind of mirror. This mirror showed me why I felt the way I did, where I was, where I'd been, and even where I might go next.

1

I was one of the many students who received report cards saying "Could do well if she applied herself and stopped daydreaming so much." Although I never learned to apply myself without daydreaming, writing helped me focus by showing me how to daydream *better*—and on paper. My stories and poems showed me I could really believe in myself and my dreams. Writing also helped me in many subjects at school, allowing me to voice my feelings about what I was learning in philosophy, history, and other classes.

Closer to home, writing showed me, a glimpse at a time, that maybe I was okay. I wrote a lot about my family—how they acted and how I *reacted*. Many times I didn't know what I truly felt until I started writing. The words I scribbled kept me from freezing up or closing myself off from the world. Writing, then and now, helped me *feel*—sometimes pain, often confusion, always doubt, and occasionally real joy.

Writing opened my heart and, in the process, I began to discover my own true self.

Writing also saved my life *for* something . . . the chance to keep writing. It gave me a way to make something that felt creative and alive—something with flesh and bones and blood that might live, like Dr. Frankenstein's monster, on its own. Most of all, writing brought me home. As I filled up journals, I felt my life had meaning. I felt I belonged and was welcome on the page. No one could ever take this away from me.

How Writing Can Save *Your* Life

Writing gives you a place to save and savor your memories and insights, your thoughts and wishes, your feelings and goals. Writing can help you create and re-create yourself. How? By sharpening your vision of who you are, what you want, and where you're going. Writing can bring you hope, help you dream wide and deep, and let you know you're not alone.

Writing can also help you express your true feelings and understand yourself better. Most of all, it can make you feel more alive.

As writer and Pulitzer Prize-winning poet Annie Dillard explains: "The line of words fingers your own heart. . . . And in your words, your own life will come, slowly or quickly, with or without much prodding, showing you your reflection." The creative process, in other words, helps you reach deep inside the place where your fears hide and your dreams dance.

You make stories or poems, or any other form of writing, by leaping out of what you thought you knew and onto the blank page where anything's possible. To engage in this process is to *create*. You aim your hand toward the paper and touch something that reaffirms the life running through your veins.

This Is Your Book

This book is for you. It can show you how to let writing heal your hurts and sing your songs. Again and again, I've seen students produce their strongest, best-crafted writing when they're sharing what they care about or what moves them. Writing becomes a way to express who they truly are and, in the process, they get to know—and like—themselves a little more.

You can use this book any way you want. Read it straight through, skip around, or go from back to front.

In Part 1, "Testing the Waters," you'll find twelve reasons why putting pen to paper is important and beneficial. You'll discover how to think like a writer and enhance your creativity. You'll also find tips on the craft of writing, so you can practice and sharpen your skills.

Part 2, "Diving into Your Life," is designed to encourage the habit of writing. You'll find writing activities that help you understand your world, yourself, your feelings, and your future. Feel free to change any of the exercises to suit your needs: you're the authority (the author) of your own writing, so you can decide what works best for you.

Part 3, "Surfacing," shows you how to revise your writing so it's as strong as possible. You'll find out why you should edit to strengthen your work, how to bring life to seemingly dead stories and poems, what to do with any lines and passages you've cut, and when to just let your writing sit and rest.

Part 4, "Swimming Toward Home," discusses the importance of connecting with other readers and writers. You'll learn about taking writing classes, participating in readings, finding mentors, joining a writer's group, and getting published. This section includes helpful information about many of the benefits and challenges of going public with your writing.

Throughout the book, you'll find samples of writing by real teens, advice and quotes from famous writers (perhaps their words can help you find *your* words), plus a wealth of resources that point the way toward books, Web sites, and other helpful tools. Think of *Write Where You Are* as a smorgasbord—you're free to sample what entices you, nourishes you, and tastes good. You can season any of the dishes to your liking. If a particular writing exercise or suggestion doesn't work for you, add a dash of your own creativity and take another taste. Go for second and third helpings of exercises you love. You can even combine the writing activities into a whole new recipe of your own. Be as creative as you can be.

If you want to write to me with comments about this book or questions about your own writing, please do. Send your mail to:

Caryn Mirriam-Goldberg
c/o Free Spirit Publishing Inc.
400 First Avenue North, Suite 616
Minneapolis, MN 55401-1724

If you're online, you can contact me at:
help4kids@freespirit.com

Your life is made up of stories and understandings, circling around the center of who you are like the rings of the heartwood of a tree. Through writing, you'll discover your ideas, your stories, who you are, and who you may become.

You'll also come to understand the power of language, of finding the right words, of speaking in your own true voice. Each poem, story, journal entry, or letter you write is part of the journey into yourself and out to the world. As Henry Miller put it: "Writing, like life itself, is a voyage of discovery."

PART 1

Testing the Waters: Discovering Yourself Through Writing

"When I'm not writing, I can't make sense out of anything. I feel the need to make some sense and find some order, and writing fiction is the only way I've found that seems to begin to do that."

ALICE MCDERMOTT

Writing is a way to make sense of and find meaning in your life. Your words can serve as a magic mirror for you, reflecting who you are, who you want to be, and who you *can* be. Through writing, you may discover more of yourself—the silent, hurt, and lonely parts, and the creative, joyful, and invincible parts. In a sense, your writing is like your thumbprint on the world: the swirls, ridges, and images identify you as *you*.

CHAPTER 1

Why Write?

When I think of what writing has given me, especially when I was tumbling through my teen years, I realize there's not a basket big enough to hold the gifts. Just sitting down in a corner and filling up my notebooks inspired me, made me feel alive, carried me through the difficult times, and showed me I had something to give to the world. Writing was a friend who would meet me on the page whenever I needed to sit and talk. Your writing can help you get inspired, too. Following are twelve good reasons to write:

> "Writing is a way of cutting away at the surface of things, of exploring, of understanding."
>
> Robert Duncan

Twelve Reasons to Write

1. Writing helps you discover who you are. When you put pen to paper and pour out your thoughts, you begin to discover what you know about yourself and the world. You can explore what you love or hate, what hurts you, what you need, what you can give, and what you want out of life. This helps you better understand yourself and your place in the world.

2. Writing can help you believe in yourself and raise your self-esteem. The very act of making something out of nothing produces a feeling of pride and a sense of accomplishment. Knowing that you're able to fill up a journal with your thoughts, write a story, or put together a research paper helps you believe in your own abilities, talents, and perseverance. Your increased self-confidence can inspire you to take more risks in your writing and in other creative activities.

3. When you write, you hear your own unique voice. Poet William Stafford once said that a writer is not someone who has something to say as much as someone who has *found a way to say it.* Writing allows you to communicate in your own words and voice, without the filters and blocks you might use when talking to people you want to please, avoid, connect with, impress, or run from. Writing also gives you an opportunity to listen to your own distinctive voice, recognize it, and know it better.

4. Writing shows you what you can give the world. As you write, you can explore your particular talents, interests, and passions. What are you good at? What do you feel compelled to throw energy into? What do you want to improve? Writing allows you to delve deeper into yourself and put into words what it is you want to be and do. It helps you find your calling.

5. As you write, you seek answers to questions and find new questions to ask. Because writing forces you to sit and think, it can be a way of finding answers to questions in your life. Writing is introspective by nature; it gives you the opportunity to carefully review choices and decisions about everything from what to study, to who to hang out with, to how to tell someone what's on your mind. In the process of writing about your issues and examining your questions, you may find answers that are right for you.

6. Writing enhances your creativity. Creating anything means asking questions, dwelling in doubt and confusion, and finally reaching a breakthrough. When you write, you immerse yourself in the creative process. The more practice you get, the more easily you can transfer these skills to other areas of your life (school, activities, a job) that require creative solutions.

7. You can share yourself with others through writing. Many people believe that the written word allows for more freedom of expression than the spoken word. Writing lets you

> "I think I did pretty well, considering I started out with nothing but a bunch of blank paper."
>
> Steve Martin

reveal aspects of yourself that don't always come across in face-to-face communication, phone conversations, or class discussions. Your writing self, in contrast to your talking self, has more time to reflect on what you believe, what you want to say, and why you think or feel a certain way.

8. Writing gives you a place to release anger, fear, sadness, and other painful feelings. Feelings are intense. They can hurt you to the core. (According to writer Oscar Wilde, their main charm is that they don't last!) When you're feeling angry, scared, upset, or depressed, it helps to get these emotions on paper rather than bottle them up. Writing is a safe way to release your feelings, explore them, and begin to cope.

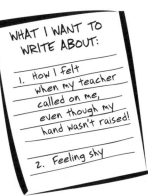

WHAT I WANT TO WRITE ABOUT:

1. How I felt when my teacher called on me, even though my hand wasn't raised!

2. Feeling shy

9. You can help heal yourself through writing. It's no secret that many writers derive at least some healing benefits from writing. Whether it's their career, passion, hobby, or all three, writing offers writers a way to examine their wounds and, if they want, share them with the world. You, too, can take what has hurt you and turn it into something that helps you. The very act of creating can be a way to heal.

10. Writing can bring you joy and a way to express it. It's fun to put into words what's important and meaningful to you, then read what you've written. But the *process* of writing can be fun, too. It's exciting to put words onto paper and fill up pages with your ideas and opinions, not knowing exactly what you're going to say or what will come next. When you allow yourself to relax and see what happens on the page, you experience the thrill of creative expression.

"I like to write when I feel spiteful; it's like having a good sneeze."

D. H. Lawrence

11. Writing can make you feel more alive. The words, the images, the delight or grief that surfaces, the discoveries, the answers or questions that come to you as you write—all of this helps you feel more alive. Writing, like any art, is a way to connect with yourself, other people, and the world. In doing so, you may feel more involved, engaged, and interested in life. You may even be compelled to embrace it wholeheartedly.

12. You can discover your dreams through writing. Through the quiet and solitary act of writing, you can discover your greatest dreams (not what you or other people *think* they should be, but what *really* calls to you). You can think about these dreams, what it would take for them to become real, and what you can do to start making things happen. Then you can write your way there.

"Lift up your eyes upon this day breaking for you. Give birth to the dream."

Maya Angelou

CHAPTER 2

Thinking Like a Writer

What does it mean to think like a writer? Writing isn't just something you do when you sit at the computer or with a journal. It's a process that awakens your creativity and strengthens your awareness of the world around you. Writing also puts you in touch with your beliefs and emotions. The more you write, the more confident you become about expressing your feelings and your unique perspective on life.

Writing Is More Than Writing

When people think of what it means to be a writer, they often imagine the *practice* of writing: the filling up of pages, the editing of paragraphs, the careful examination of words. This *is* all part of writing, which at its heart is a practice of putting pen to paper or fingers to keyboard. But it's also more.

Being a writer, thinking like a writer, means integrating the creative process into your entire life. Author Jamaica Kincaid says she's always writing in her mind, especially when she's gardening. By the time she actually puts pen to paper, she has already composed her stories many times in her head. Joyce Carol Oates, another contemporary author, believes " . . . no matter what you are doing, driving a car or walking or doing housework . . . you can still be writing." Writing, then, is a process of observing, thinking, creating, reflecting—and writing it all down.

> "It is by sitting down to write every morning that one becomes a writer. Those who do not do this remain amateurs."
>
> Gerald Brenan

Sometimes writing can be routine. You may jot words in a journal or on scraps of paper, just to get in the habit of writing. At other times, you may sit down to write because you feel a burst of inspiration. Either way, when writing becomes a habit—something you do nearly every day or several times a week—it seeps into your life and flavors how you perceive the world. Only then do you truly become a writer.

I once asked a teacher of mine who was an accomplished novelist, "Can I be a writer if I don't write?" After all, I thought, I write in my head, think like a writer, and believe in the power of words. He listened to me and then shook his head. "No," he replied. "To be a writer, you have to write."

So write. Even if you're scared. Even if you're sure you'll write "garbage." The more you write, the more you'll think of yourself as a writer. In the words of poet Annie Dillard, "The page, the page, that eternal blankness" is what will teach you to write. You learn by doing. Words lead to more words.

Aim past the blankness of the page and straight into the heart of what you have to say. All you have to do is start.

 **Write Now...**

To get started, write your response to one or more of the following questions. There's no "right" way to answer any of them. Imagine each question as a doorway for you to pass through and explore what's on the other side. What surprises do you find when you enter?

- Why might you want to write?
- Do you consider yourself a writer? Why or why not?
- Why is writing important?
- What is it that writing brings you or that you want it to bring you?
- What could writing do for you? What *has* it done for you?
- What do you most want to write about? Why?

I want to write because I have stories in me. I
dream stories, I think stories, I carry stories in
me just like my veins carry my blood. I want to
tell these stories.

While I don't tell people I'm a writer, I kind of
think I might be one. It just sounds like too much
to say it, but inside, I've always been thinking
up stories and telling them to myself. And I write
down all I can, so doesn't that make me a writer?

Leigh, 15

Be an Observer

When I decided I wanted to be a writer, I happened to read
somewhere about the importance of writers being good
observers. Taking this to heart, I started observing as fiercely
(and ridiculously) as I could. Riding the school bus, I'd watch
how the shapes of bare branches were etched upon the sky.
Lying on the ground, I sought out stories to explain why the
clouds were in whatever surrealistic shape they had taken at
that moment. Sitting on plastic-covered couches at crowded
family gatherings, I listened to the conversations of my relatives, paying close attention to how often they used the word
aggravation and memorizing the looks of exasperation they gave
one another.

Sometimes I'd fill my journals with pages of tedious and
silly details—the pattern of my uncle's tie took thirty lines to
describe; the angle of chair legs became a source of great fasci-
nation and many words. Truly, what I wrote was often so mind-
numbingly boring that even *I* couldn't bear to read it. And yet,
in the act of watching and listening carefully, and writing about
the details, I learned to see and hear much more than I would
have otherwise.

Years later, when teachers beamed at me and asked, "How
did you come up with this image?" or "How do you write such

" ...keep your
eyes open. Notice
what's going on
around you."

William Burroughs

believable dialogue?" I couldn't really explain. The answer was rooted in the many hours I'd spent breaking down the details and adding them up in my own words to create a bigger picture.

When you sharpen your senses, you become more aware of the fine details that comprise the big picture around you. And in seeing, hearing, and experiencing so much so vividly, you discover a wealth of material to draw from. You may wonder, where do writers get their ideas? Where do they get their images, dialogue, rhythms, surprising plot turns, and fully developed characters? From years of watching and listening closely. From being as awake as possible, as often as possible.

It's essential for you, as a writer, to be mindful of all that goes on around you. Occasionally, pretend your eyes are a movie camera, first taking in the large vistas, then focusing in on people, objects, gestures, and conversations. Notice all that the little lift of a hand or turn of a phrase can tell you about what and who you're watching and hearing. In your mind, narrate the stories as they unfold.

A lot of material exists in your own mind, too, which is undoubtedly well furnished with memories, experiences, ideas, and feelings. Take note of the physical sensations you have: they may be telling you something about your emotions. (For example, if your stomach drops every time a certain person enters the room, this certainly tells you something about your feelings.) Through your own responses—those of your body, mind, and heart—you can learn volumes about yourself.

Watch carefully. Listen. Feel. A lot is happening everywhere all the time. The more you take notice of what's around you— what you see, hear, touch, taste, smell—the more you can draw from your observations to make your writing fresh.

> "Everything a writer experiences as a young person goes into the later writing in some form."
>
> Lois Lowry

> "I dwell in possibility."
>
> Emily Dickinson

Dare to Be Creative

What does it mean to be creative? Maybe it's expressing yourself through some kind of art like writing, dance, sculpture, or music. Or letting your imagination roam, following impulses, trusting hunches, and seeing possibilities. Perhaps it's simply the act of bringing something new into being.

Do you think you're creative? According to authors Daniel Goleman, Paul Kaufman, and Michael Ray in their book *The Creative Spirit,* creativity is something "half the world thinks of as a mysterious quality that the other half possesses." Yet *everyone* has creativity. (They just don't always know it or act on it!) It takes creativity to write a poem, paint a picture, or invent something new; in the process, you think originally, use your imagination, ask questions, seek answers, and solve problems your own way. This is the essence of creativity.

Dr. Teresa Amabile, an author and creativity expert, says the creative process involves several ingredients. First, you need to have *passion,* or the urge to do something you love. Passion is the force that fuels the desire to create. Do you have a passion to write? If you do, nothing will stop you. You'll write not for rewards, grades, recognition, or to please someone—but because you get personal satisfaction from it.

You also need *domain skills,* meaning talent or ability in your area of interest. If you want to be a writer, you can start by learning some of the basic techniques of writing, such as being descriptive, honing your personal voice, and finding the right tone for your work. With practice, your skills will improve.

Another ingredient is *creative thinking,* which means using your imagination and taking risks to make something you haven't made before. It takes courage to write, to express yourself in words. Being a writer is a brave act.

Here are some tips to help you become a more creative writer:

1. Risk beginning. It's often easier to clean your closet, wash the car, and make five dozen blueberry pancakes than it is to start writing. Writers—young and old, famous or not—sometimes have trouble getting inspired. You may tell yourself now is not the "right time" to write, or you're not in a writing mood, or you don't have the "right" pen. But if you hang around all day

> "The artist is driven by passion; and passion most powerfully derives from our own experiences and memories."
>
> Joyce Carol Oates

16

waiting for lightning to strike, your page will stay blank. Believe in what you have to say and start filling up the empty pages with your words.

2. Don't make each word feel like it's under surveillance. Most writers, most of the time, write bad first drafts. If you harshly judge your first draft, or even your first line, the second draft (or line) won't want to show its scared little face. Be gentle with the fragile starts of new writing. Tell yourself you're just going to fill up some pages with words. Don't expect sudden grandeur, but don't assume instant defeat either. You may *want* to grow a prize orchid, but that kind of pressure can make it hard to produce even a dandelion.

3. Follow your writing. You might intend to write about your crush on X, only to find you're exploring how you can't stand Y. If your hand feels compelled to write certain things, let it lead you. The best part of the creative process is the constant surprise.

"To write is to write is to write is to write is to write is to write is to write is to write."

Gertrude Stein

 **Write Now...**

One way to unleash your creativity is by *freewriting,* which disciplines you to sit for a predetermined length of time (usually ten minutes) and write without stopping. You can write about whatever pops into your head—a dream you had the night before or the new CD you want to buy, for example. The point is to get the wheels in motion.

Sit down and start writing whatever's on your mind—whatever crawls down your arm, through your fingertips, and onto the page. Don't stop for at least ten minutes. Keep your hand moving, even if you can't think of anything

to write except "Why am I writing this?" or "Can't think, can't think, can't think" over and over. If you have a hard time coming up with a topic, try one of these:

- What did you see today? (Or what *didn't* you see today?)
- If you had a twin, what would she or he be like? (And if you *have* a twin, write about what life would be like if only one— or three!—had been born at once.)
- Where would you travel if you could go anywhere? What would you do there?

If I had a twin, she would be totally different from me. Instead of being sloppy, she would be neat. She would line her shoes up in her closet each night, and everything else would be hung or folded neatly. She would have her makeup in a special case, sorted by color and type. She would be . . . can't think, can't think . . . just like me, I mean, she would look just like me, but she would dress differently. She would wear khakis (I hate khakis!) with button-down shirts and new white sandals. And she wouldn't look like a nerd. My twin would be stuck-up. She would tell people she was better than me. She would make fun of my clothing and my room. She would say my friends weren't as good as hers. She would be very demanding and talk on the phone for hours. She would yell at me to feed the dog. She would wear pink nail polish and act like she was older than me. She would always be very competitive with me.

Gwen, 15

"You have to find the key, the clue. In language all you have are those 26 letters, some punctuation and some paper."

Toni Morrison

One of the benefits of freewriting is that words appear on the page: suddenly your ideas, images, and descriptions are right in front of you. Even if all you come up with are random phrases and fragments of ideas, you've accomplished something!

The next step is to expand your freewriting and help it take shape (kind of like adding water to a sponge). One way is to choose a few of the more interesting words or phrases you've written and *brainstorm,* or make a list of new ideas that occur to you, and go from there.

PHRASES:
- Keeps closet and shoes and makeup neat
- Wears khakis, button-down shirts, white sandals
- tells people she's better than me
- makes fun of my clothing and room

NEW IDEAS:
- very organized
- gets job I didn't get at café
- buys car with money she makes
- keeps car neat
- doesn't let me drive it
- acts like we're not related

Did You Know?

Another way to enhance your writing is through *clustering,* which is similar to brainstorming. Developed by writer and researcher Gabriele Lusser Rico in her book *Writing the Natural Way,* clustering is a technique that helps you "grow" your writing in many ways at once by taking an idea and branching off in new directions. To cluster, select one word from your freewriting and circle it on the center of a new page: this is your *seed word* Next, jot down all kinds of related words as they occur to you. Circle each one and draw lines between ideas you can link together.

Seed word: Competition

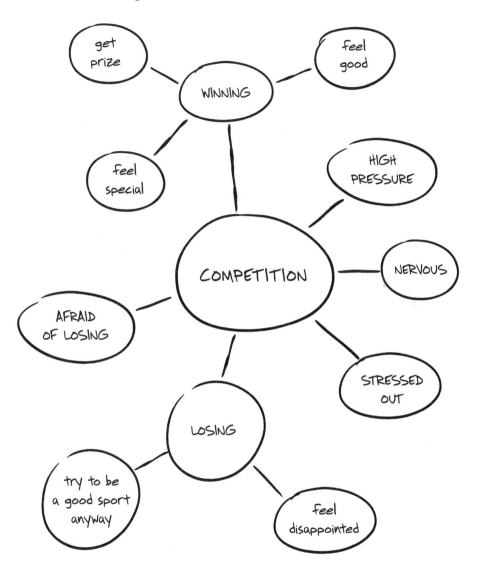

Think of your seed word as a tree that grows branches that in turn grow leaves, or even blossoms and fruit. Limb by limb, you branch into new territory, finding new places to reach and grow in your writing. Eventually, you have a visual picture of new ideas to explore.

One other method of developing your writing is through *sorting*. If you ever watched *Sesame Street* as a kid, you may remember a song about sorting that said "one of these things is not like the other" and asked you to find the object that didn't fit with the rest. In the creative sense, sorting is grouping like with like—it's a way to take all your ideas and words, and see what relates to what.

WHY I WOULD DISLIKE MY TWIN:

VERY NEAT:

- keeps closet neat
- keeps makeup neat
- keeps car neat
- dresses neat

VERY COMPETITIVE WITH ME:

- gets job I wanted
- doesn't share with me or help me
- makes fun of my room, clothes
- tells people we're not related
- tries to get me in trouble

COMPETITION MAKES ME FEEL:

- nervous
- afraid of losing
- stressed out
- under pressure

LOSING MAKES ME FEEL:

- disappointed in myself
- like I have to act nice to the winner

If you had created these lists, you'd have many idea-starters. You could write a story about your imaginary twin who keeps messing up your life. Or a twin who's always competing with you and winning. Or how one day *you* win and how this makes your twin feel. Brainstorming, clustering, and sorting are great ways to boost your creativity and explore new directions in your writing.

 WRITER'S CORNER

The Creative Spirit by Daniel Goleman, Paul Kaufman, and Michael Ray (New York: Dutton, 1992). Creativity is something *everyone* can develop. This companion volume to the PBS television series draws on the wisdom of Japanese Zen masters, maverick entrepreneurs, and leading inventors to show how creativity can improve the quality of anybody's life.

Writing the Natural Way by Gabriele Lusser Rico (Los Angeles: J. P. Tarcher, 1983). This book shows how writing can be as natural as telling a story to a friend, and as easy as daydreaming.

Get Past the Creativity Guard Dogs

Writing is like planting a garden. You start with nothing but the seeds of an idea and the determination to make something grow. You nurture what blooms, weed out what doesn't belong, and after all your effort, you enjoy the fruits of your labor. In other words, you give life to a poem, an essay, a song, or another piece without knowing beforehand exactly how it will turn out. You have to trust the process.

But sometimes your creativity is blocked, making it hard, or impossible, to create. When this happens, you need to find a way to get past your brain's "guard dogs": the pit bull of control and the basset hound of inertia. The pit bull wants everything neat and orderly, protected, and readily defendable. The basset hound wants to roll over and be loved. Who can blame either of them? They just want comfort and security.

Suppose you start writing and the pit bull jumps up and down barking. He says your work is too messy, boring, silly, imperfect, or wrong. He threatens to bite you, and he fights you every step of the way.

To get past the pit bull, you have to be willing to make a mess. Write whatever comes to mind, and don't worry if it's not perfect. Be sloppy, ignore the rules of grammar and punctuation, color outside the lines. Let yourself write a whole lot of "junk" without being critical of the "mess" you're making. Afterward, carefully sift through your work. You'll probably find a few treasures.

> "Write freely and as rapidly as possible and throw the whole thing on paper. Never correct or rewrite until the whole thing is down."
>
> John Steinbeck

Writers (even the famous ones) often start by scribbling their ideas, emotions, and random thoughts on the page without worrying about how "good" or "bad" the words are. You can do this, too.

What if it's not the pit bull you're dealing with but the basset hound? This dog is tired, afraid, and worn out. He just wants to be fed a sweet bone upon a down pillow. As soon as you start to do something artistic, he whimpers and rolls over. The basset hound wants you to forget about taking any creative risks. Eventually, this dog has to learn to stand on all four legs and trot into the world.

If you want to create something, it's time to say good-bye to your furry canine friends. Tell them to sit. Keep them at bay. Every time they bark, whimper, whine, or growl, throw them some bones to chew and cushions to sleep on. Once you venture past the guard dogs, you can cruise down your own creative path.

> "Nothing you write, if you hope to be any good, will ever come out as you first hoped."
>
> Lillian Hellman

WRITER'S CORNER

The Artist's Way: A Spiritual Path to Higher Creativity by Julia Cameron (New York: Putnam, 1992). This book takes readers through a self-directed twelve-week writing program designed to dissolve blocks and recover creativity. It's especially useful for writers who feel they have lost some of their ability to create and want help getting it back.

Write Now...

Is a guard dog (or another "animal") getting in your way? Here's how to find out:

▪ Make a list of the things that prevent you from writing what you want, how you want, when you want (for example, "No time" or "I'm too busy" or "I'm feeling lazy right now").

▪ Imagine these excuses as pesky animals. What creatures do you see? A white rabbit who's always running late? A busy beaver? A sloth? Why do these creatures act this way? Which one best represents your creative block?

- Ask yourself how you might find a way to adopt this creature and take such good care of it that it would no longer get in your way. What would you feed it? Where would it sleep? You can even draw the creature, cut it out, and keep it with your writing materials (think of it as your "pet peeve"). Anytime you find yourself making the same old excuses, pull out your pet and find out what it needs. Then take care of it, so you can write.

My creature is a camel with one hump. She seems
gentle, able to walk long distances without a
drink, and generally pretty nice. The only problem
is that her hump is high up and sort of pointed on
top, making it hard for me to climb up on her and
stay there.

    I think this is because I have so much trouble
getting started on any writing. I want it to be so
good—so "high up" in quality—that a lot of times
I can't get anything out at all. I write a line,
cross it out, write it again, cross it out, etc.

    The good thing is that once I do get started,
then I can go a long way without resting. I can
write for an hour or so until I've crossed to the
other side of the story or essay.

    So maybe having a camel isn't so bad after all.

                                        Delores, 17

Did You Know?

In 1935, e. e. cummings published *No Thanks* and dedicated it to fourteen publishers who had rejected it.

Zap the Creativity Zappers

Creativity expert Dr. Teresa Amabile describes five creativity zappers: *surveillance, evaluation, rewards, pressure,* and *competition.* Looking over this list, you'll see that all of the zappers have to do with judgments, which have a way of stifling creativity.

    For example, if you're competing for an award, your writing might be influenced by the knowledge that a judge will evaluate your work. If you worry that anyone reading your work is

"Creation is
everything you do.
Make something."

Ntozake Shange

going to be critical of it, this might make *you* more critical of it, too. There's nothing like a bunch of judges to make it hard to do anything—hard to get started and hard to appreciate what you've done.

After you write something and you read over it, what happens? Does a familiar, not-so-welcome voice tell you your work is no good? Maybe the voice is a mere whisper saying, "I'm not so sure you can be a writer." Or maybe the voice thunders and booms, "YOU CAN'T DO ANYTHING RIGHT!" The good (and bad) news is that *everyone* has judges or voices inside saying words like *can't, shouldn't, mustn't,* and *don't.* You're not alone.

Some judges speak in familiar voices. In fact, some can sound exactly like an uncle who once told your parents you would never amount to anything. Others do a mean imitation of that cruel eighth-grade teacher who said you wrote like a fifth grader. But some voices can't be traced back to specific people or events: these voices are fueled by disbelief in yourself.

What the judges (*your* judges) do is judge. While doing so, they make it hard for you to write. Just try to write a poem with someone standing over your shoulder, watching your every move, analyzing each word, and making strange little grunts of disapproval. This is what it's like to write with judges breathing down your neck.

New writing is like a creature coming into existence. Word by word, cell by cell, it forms. It's raw and tender and requires love and protection. Thin-skinned and sensitive, it needs a long time before it's ready to be born and meet the critics. In fact, if it's not protected, fed, and nurtured, this writing-creature may shrivel up and disappear.

Think of your new writing as a baby mouse: blind, hairless, and lost without its mother. Think of your judges as a big hungry cat. You can imagine what will happen if you don't protect your new writing from the judges.

So shake these creativity stiflers off your tail and out of your way. It may not be easy, because judges are used to pounding their gavels and having people take their decisions and proclamations seriously. Judges don't go away readily or willingly.

How do you ditch them? One way is to invent a comfortable and inviting vehicle to transport them to a faraway place. Think of it as sending the judges out for pizza, in Italy of course, so they'll be gone a long, long time. Describe the vehicle and how it will transport them to Rome in search of the best pizza on the planet. (You know how fussy judges can be—they could be gone for years hunting down the perfect pizza!) Have fun imagining how the judges are dressed, what they say to each other, how they act, and what they think about the journey.

You could even send the judges on a bus trip to . . . nowhere. It will take an eternity for them to reach their destination, so enjoy waving good-bye as the bus pulls away, the smell of diesel fuel and freedom in the air.

```
My judges are on the train to nowhere. They boarded
just outside my bedroom window, all twenty of them.
Some of them were short with mean, bunched-up
faces. Some were tall and angular-looking, and they
were always shaking their fingers at me and saying,
"Tsk, tsk." Other judges screamed nonstop, things
like "You're so stupid," and "You're stupid-looking,
too."
    I hated my judges. That's why when the train
arrived, I woke them all up, the ones asleep under
my bed, the bunches of them in my closets (between
hangers with clothes on them, where they'd insult
my wardrobe all night), and the ones hiding in
drawers. One big judge with red eyes was under my
pillow. I told them to hurry up or they would be
late for the train, saying, "I know how much you
guys hate to be late; you're so afraid you'll miss
something to insult."
    "Where is the train going?" they wailed.
    "Nowhere I can say," I answered.
    "Why should we go?" they cried.
    "Because if you don't, you'll miss out on
EVERYTHING!!!"
    That got them going. They boarded the train,
```

"A writer needs to be doubtful, questioning. I write out of curiosity and bewilderment . . . I've learned a lot I could not have learned if I were not a writer."

William Trevor

> and it left the station. I stood and waved good-
> bye, knowing that nowhere was very far away and
> the judges would probably have to travel the rest
> of my life to get there.
>
> Chad, 16

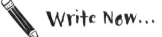 ## Write Now...

To free yourself from the power of your personal judges, take a blank piece of paper, set a timer for five to ten minutes, and write every negative thought that floats into your mind about your writing, yourself, and your life. Write with abandon. Don't worry about grammar, spelling, punctuation, or sense. If you get stuck, write "Can't think, can't think, can't think" until more words flop their way onto your paper.

When time's up, tear the paper into tiny pieces. Tell the judges, "You had your say, but I don't have to keep you around." Ripping up all those negative statements about yourself will help clear the critical voices from your head.

What do you do with the torn-up paper? Throw the pieces in the trash, bury them, or scatter them around your room like confetti (this is a celebration, after all). Then take a deep breath, relax, and start writing other things.

> "One does not discover new lands without consenting to lose sight of the shore for a very long time."
>
> André Gide

Let Go

Creating something is an amazing experience. You simply begin without knowing what the result will be. As you continue moving your hand across the page (or computer keyboard), something magical happens. A piece of writing is born.

You may look at your creation afterward and be surprised it didn't turn out as you'd imagined. All kinds of wonderful things can occur when you're not exactly sure what you're doing, so give yourself some space to let your mind wander. Nineteenth-century poet John Keats called this *negative capability,* or the ability to be in a place of no answers without trying to force answers. In other words, you wander confused in a haze of doubt until you reach a destination.

Sometimes you'll find that a piece of writing seems to have its own intentions. This is the mystery of the creative process. You write (draw, paint, sculpt) half thinking, half not-thinking, and somehow the deepest intention of the piece makes itself known.

So as you write, hold on to and let go of your writing. It sounds like a contradiction, but it's really not. Hold on to what you're writing, and keep your eyes open for opportunities to let your writing grow into something bigger than you originally imagined. At the same time, let go of steering each word, so moments of illumination may sneak up and surprise you.

Many scholars in the field of psychology have found that people who create or perform at their peak experience something called a *white moment* where everything clicks, and what they create feels harmonious and effortless. In such a moment, they exceed their usual limits and venture beyond the boundaries of their mind to a state Zen Buddhists call *no-mind.* To experience this sense of clarity, you have to be willing to let yourself go—to write without judging, worrying, or holding yourself back.

In a moment of intense creativity, you allow yourself to be guided by intuition—the source of insight inside you that sees new possibilities in your writing. You resist forcing your words to stand at attention and, instead, set them free to wander, ramble, drift, and perhaps even dance.

If it's hard for you to write and let go, try the following techniques, which free you to think and write in new directions.

- Before you write, sit in a chair with your hands resting on your lap. Tense your legs, arms, feet, and hands all at once, and hold this pose for five seconds. Then relax, take a deep breath, and tense and relax your muscles several more times. Now start writing.

- Put on some music that really speaks to you (headphones are great for this because they envelop you in music), and then freewrite about whatever topic comes to mind. After a song or two, review your freewriting, and circle a few phrases you like.

"It's one of the things I do as a writer: I attempt to hook in, and then I relax and let the rest of me tell me what to do—sort of like those mad scientist's hands that get attached to the innocent person's body."

Cynthia Voigt

Next, pick one of these phrases and place it at the top of a new page. Start writing about whatever comes to mind now, with or without the music moving you along.

• Play a musical instrument, dance wildly to music you love, or draw a picture with crayons, pastels, or colored pencils. Now, without stopping to think about what you've played or danced or drawn, go straight to the page or screen and start writing. See what comes when your mind and body are still influenced by another art form.

• When you wake up in the morning, pick up a journal you've placed beside your bed the night before and start writing about what you dreamt or what you feel at that moment. Write for about five minutes (or more, if you'd like), and then read what you've written. Are you inspired to continue?

• Take a long walk, and when you find a comfortable place, sit down and write for five minutes about whatever comes to mind. (This may be harder to do in winter or rainy weather, but it's still possible.)

• Right before you go to sleep, write in a journal. Don't read what you wrote until the next morning. See if your words stir you to write some more.

• Take a piece of freewriting you've done, and copy or type it over again, half paying attention and half not paying attention. Change a word here or there if it seems to fit, and see what you can create.

Tell Your Truth

Being a writer often means journeying far into the center of yourself. Some of what you find there may shake, stir, anger, or shock you.

Writing about your innermost feelings, ideas, perceptions, hopes, and fears means telling the truth about who you are, even (and especially) if you're just writing for yourself. Telling the truth as you understand it means writing honestly about an experience and how it affected you, without holding back. The

> "We do not write in order to be understood; we write in order to understand."
>
> C. Day Lewis

> "My writing has been very autobiographical. The events are true to me. They may not be true to other people."
>
> Jamaica Kincaid

truth here is *your* truth. It's what contains meaning, power, and promise for *you*.

Often, it's difficult to get to the heart of what you really want, or need, to say. You may feel embarrassed to write about your true feelings or events that caused you pain. You may think, "What if someone reads this? What if someone decides I'm crazy or weird because of this?" These are the judges in your head coming back to bother you. (To read more about judges and how to deal with them, see "Zap the Creativity Zappers" on pages 23–26.) Remember, your writing can be just for you—no one else ever has to read it. If you want, hide your personal writing in a place that only you know about.

Writing can help you journey through old pain to a place of new understanding, courage, and strength. But you have to face what hurts you—and be willing to spill it out onto the page. Following are some tips for telling the truth in your writing and taking care of yourself when writing hurts.

1. Explore your feelings honestly. Like everyone else in the world, you may sometimes experience moments when you question your worth. You might feel like everything is going wrong and everything you do seems to make things worse. During such times, writing might be just what you need to lift yourself up. As you write, you may find new ways to express your emotions, think through choices, and come up with solutions. Seeing things on paper, or just taking the time to think and write, helps you put life in perspective.

2. Write in third person. Writing about painful subjects is sometimes more bearable when you write in the third person ("she" or "he" instead of "I"). Calling yourself he or she, or renaming yourself Marvin or Lillian, creates some distance between you and the pain of what you're writing. And it may bring you a wider view.

3. Take a break. You can also choose to stop writing about something, put it on a shelf, and come back to it when you're ready. There's no pressure to show anyone or to resolve any problems right this moment.

"Though life may be painful, there is a joy and a power in writing, even when you're dealing with something that is hard to live through day by day. You're trying to understand what you're living through by using the tools of words and images and the beautiful inner structure of language."

Sandra McPherson

30

"It always comes
back to the same
necessity: go
deep enough
and there is a
bedrock of truth,
however hard."

May Sarton

If you feel overwhelmed or stuck, stop for a while and do something physical like walk, bike, in-line skate, practice karate, work out, swim, dance to your favorite music, or even jump up and down screaming out ways to conjugate French verbs. When you do a physical activity, you give your overwrought mind a break. Exercising, even for just a few minutes, releases endorphins, or brain chemicals, that give you a natural high. You'll feel refreshed and relaxed when you return to your writing.

4. Get support. Writing alone can't solve every problem, so you might need to get help from an adult. Talk to your family, a teacher, a religious advisor, a youth group leader, or a school counselor about whatever is hurting or angering you. Or look for sources of support within your community: mental health centers or teen clinics sometimes charge clients on a sliding-scale fee (you pay only what you can afford to pay). You may also find a crisis hotline listed in your Yellow Pages.

If you decide to see a counselor, it may be helpful to keep a journal while you're working through problems. As you write, you can explore your feelings, which helps you build trust and self-esteem. Studies have shown that writing helps people feel better both emotionally *and* physically—it really does have a therapeutic effect!

Encourage and Praise Yourself

"I write to clear
my own mind, to
find out what I
think and feel."

V. S. Pritchett

The phrase "willing suspension of disbelief" is often used to instruct people to drop their tight hold on reality long enough to read something and believe that it's true—even if it seems impossible. For example, if you read science fiction or fantasy books, you need to willingly suspend your disbelief so you can temporarily accept that people are able to turn into vapor, fly to other galaxies, and rehydrate themselves into humans again. Pretending anything is possible makes reading the story more meaningful.

The same is true for your view of yourself, as a writer and as a person. One of the most important things you can ever do is *believe in yourself*. When you feel confident and assured, you're more likely to see positive results.

If you don't yet believe in yourself, if you don't yet believe you're a writer who has anything worthy to say, *pretend* you do anyway. Why? Because doubting yourself makes you afraid to try. When you predict failure, you're more likely to give up because you think you already know the outcome. When you predict success, on the other hand, you're more likely to put forth your best effort and accomplish what you set out to do.

So set the stage for success by encouraging yourself with praise from . . . who else? Yourself!

To see yourself in the best possible light, write down ten positive things about yourself. Study the list and store it where you can find it anytime you need a self-esteem boost. Tell yourself every day that you're creative, intelligent, and potentially great. Offering yourself praise—and sincerely believing you have something to say—will encourage you to keep writing and dreaming. Believing in oneself is a part of any artist's path.

Did You Know?

Frank Baum, creator of *The Wizard of Oz*, came up with the name "Oz" after looking at the drawer of his file cabinet that contained the letters O–Z.

 **Write Now...**

Write a letter to yourself from yourself, or from someone who loves you more than any other person in the world. This person can be anyone, real or imaginary, human or beyond human. It can even be from more than one person, if you want. The letter writer, whoever it may be, should be someone who sees you in the brightest light, believes in you from afar, and loves you unconditionally. Writing and reading this letter can help you feel more confident about yourself and your abilities.

"You have brains in your head. You have feet in your shoes. You can steer yourself any direction you choose."

Dr. Seuss

Dear Me,

How are you? You look great today—your hair, your clothes, everything. You just look real good and happy, and that makes me happy because I want the best for you. You see, I know that no matter what you do wrong in life, you're still a very fine person inside. I know that you're much smarter than you act and that sometimes you hide your ideas because you're afraid of what people will think. I know that you're very kind, too, and that you feel deeply for other people, especially those you love.

There's something else I know—that you're a good writer. Yes, you! I read that poem you wrote yesterday, and I almost cried because it was so good. And I just loved the play you wrote last summer.

So keep writing. Don't let your fears stop you. And if you get lonely, write to me. I'll always be here for you.

Love,
Me

Cara, 16

"It is of practical value to learn to like yourself. Since you must spend so much time with yourself you might as well get some satisfaction out of the relationship."

Norman Vincent Peale

Maybe you're still tempted to criticize yourself for everything—for wearing the wrong thing, saying something stupid, missing an easy answer, or even getting an annoying tune stuck in your head. Maybe you tell yourself on a regular basis, "My writing stinks!"

What can help? Sometimes you just need the words of people who love you, believe in you, or see in you something strong and true. In my bottom desk drawer, I have a manila folder full of positive job evaluations, complimentary letters from teachers, thank-you notes from students, and other reminders from people who have believed in me and in what I've tried to accomplish. In short, it's a file full of praise for myself. It may seem somewhat egotistical to save these things, but my impulse to keep kind words close at hand comes from years of not believing in myself.

I keep these letters because they're tangible evidence that someone thought I was good at something. I read through them whenever I have serious doubts about whether I'm good enough. The people who wrote the letters saw me in a brighter light than I could see myself. If I approach my writing holding that light over the page, I find that I can believe in myself enough to get out the first word, then the first sentence, and soon the first paragraph.

You, too, can put together a folder full of praise for yourself—or even a shoe box decorated with sequins, glitter, or any other materials. You can also keep a special notebook for this purpose. This folder, box, or notebook will hold letters and notes from people who have acknowledged your unique talents.

You might even make a list of the kind things people have said to you over the years. For example, maybe a teacher remarked, "You have a great writing style," or a coach told you, "You've contributed so much to the team," or a grandparent announced, "You are the most beautiful, charming, brilliant grandchild in the universe!" Write these things down. Call it your *applause list,* or whatever you want. When you're feeling down or uncertain, pull out this list and remind yourself just how great you are.

Writing is personal and intimate, and no one knows or understands your writing better than you. This is why you have to serve as your own best critic—keep cheering yourself on so you're motivated to write. Encourage yourself, praise yourself, and, most of all, believe in yourself. This helps bring out the best in your writing.

> "When you do something you are proud of, praise yourself for it."
>
> Mildred Newman

CHAPTER 3

Tools of the Trade

Of all the arts, writing is one of the most portable. Unlike dance or theater, writing doesn't require a stage. Unlike painting, it doesn't require paint, brushes, or a canvas. Unlike playing the piano, it doesn't require a piano. You can write almost anywhere, without too many people lifting their eyebrows in approval or disapproval. All you need is a pen and paper (or a computer, if you prefer) and, of course, your imagination.

But there are some other basic tools that can help you become a better writer—everything from a journal, to a library of resources, to a list of literary terms writers need to know. This chapter helps you gather the tools of the trade and put them to use.

> "Wherever I can find a place to sit down and write, that is my home."
>
> Mary TallMountain

Find a Writing Place

In high school, I did a lot of writing between classes, while sitting in the hall. I wrote while waiting for the bus, riding in the car, or sitting on the floor of my bedroom staring at a huge mess no mortal could clean alone. I felt comfortable writing just about anywhere, anytime.

Yet, it does help to have a special place to write. You can make your own space simply by choosing the place that chooses *you*—the place where you're the most relaxed and productive. Where do you feel comfortable, welcome, and safe?

Your writing place can be public, like a booth in a diner, or private, like your bedroom. If you have a place of your own to write, you also have a place that *prompts* you to write. Places, like songs or scents, can ignite the memory of what you did the last time you were there. So if you have a certain desk in the library, a corner in your house, a table at a coffee shop, or a spot beneath a tree where you like to write, each time you sit there you'll remember the act of writing and find yourself wanting to write again.

For example, I have a table in a local café where I regularly sit, drink some tea and eat a bagel, look at newspapers, and then remember that I came there to write—so I do. When I was a teenager, I had a favorite hallway in high school where I'd lean in a quiet corner, lockers looming above me, and write. Whenever I sat on those gray tiles with my back against a brick wall, I felt that I was home. This was my time and place to write.

Many writers have special writing places that help them make the most of their creativity. Katherine Paterson, author of more than twenty-five children's books, writes in a secluded getaway, an upstairs study under the eaves of her home where there's no phone and no way to hear the doorbell. Nineteenth-century novelist Jane Austen wrote at a simple pine table. Jean Craighead George, author of Newbery Medal-winner *Julie of the Wolves* and many other books, wakes up at 5:30 A.M. to write in a study that has many windows and maps. E. B. White wrote one of the best-loved children's books of all time, *Charlotte's Web,* at a little desk in a converted boathouse, which he called his "haven."

A writer may write at the same time each morning, after-noon, or evening, or write late into the night. No matter when you prefer to write, make sure you keep the time open. Mark it on your calendar or in your day planner so you remember. Perhaps your writing time begins when you wake up, or maybe you write just before bed twice a week. You may want to set aside time during the afternoon on certain days of the week,

"I surround myself with objects that carry with them a personal history— old books, bowls and boxes, splintering chairs and benches from imperial China."

Amy Tan

> "If I could I would always work in silence and obscurity, and let my efforts be known by their results."
>
> Emily Brontë

and write for longer periods on the weekends. Do whatever works for you. When you keep time open for your writing, and honor the time, you'll find a way to welcome the creative ideas that choose to visit you.

Think of your writing time as the ultimate time for yourself: time to think, heal, dream, invent, and create.

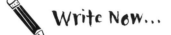 Write Now...

Think about where you like to write and the environment that makes you the most productive. Where's your *ideal* writing space? Is it outdoors under a weeping willow? Or do you prefer a private room like a den, an office, an attic, or a bedroom? How about a busy café, where you wear headphones and listen to your favorite music? Or during the bus ride to school? What do you sit on? The ground, a chair, a mound of cushions? Is your writing place quiet or noisy? Are other people nearby and, if so, what are they doing? When you think about this ideal place, how do you feel? What can you do to make this dream place real?

Did You Know?

The final words of author Gertrude Stein were, "What is the answer?" and after a long pause she asked, "But what, then, is the question?"

My favorite place is a corner of my high school where I sometimes sit after school, leaning on the cool white bricks under the lockers. I like the quiet there, the dim light, the window that looks out on the lawn. I like that it doesn't look out on a playground or parking lot or place where lots of people go, but instead just a little green hardly anyone sees.

I like to sit on my gray sweatshirt and write in my journal. Sometimes I write about what happened that day. Mostly I write about whatever nonsense crosses my mind. I write and write, and no one knows where I am to come bother me.

Cara, 16

Get a Journal

Journals are places where you can grow your writing. Think of your journal as an incubator or a greenhouse: it's the place to nurture your creations. You're free to dream on the page, work out problems, and write whatever you want.

In your journal, you can write about your thoughts, feelings, and goals. You can add inspiring quotes or cut out meaningful pictures from magazines and glue them to the journal pages. Whenever you want, you can flip through your journal and see where you've been, how you felt when you were there, what your dreams were, and how you wrote about your life.

Journals are wonderful protectors of your memories, too. You can capture the details of an important conversation, event, or moment. You'll not only record your life but also practice your skills as an observer and thinker. Regular journal writing is a good way to gain more control of your use of language and to hone your skills as a writer.

What kind of journal should you use? Many different kinds are available: legal pads, spiral notebooks, blank books, lined books, small tuck-in-your-pocket journals, album-size books. Or you can keep your journal on a computer or laptop. It's up to you.

Once you've chosen your first journal, take it for a "test drive." Do you like the way it handles? Does it feel safe? Does it feel like "you"? If you prefer another kind of journal (one that's more colorful or roomy, for example), trade it in for a new model.

Don't forget to choose your favorite writing instrument—pen, pencil, marker, or whatever. What feels best in your hand and helps you write fast and furious? You may have to try out a few pens before you find the one that feels most at home in your hand.

 WRITER'S CORNER

A Book of Your Own: Keeping a Diary or Journal by Carla Stevens (New York: Clarion Books, 1993). This book describes how to create and keep journals, with lots of intriguing examples from famous and not-so-famous people's journals.

> "I carry my journal with me almost all the time. If I have poems that just come, I write them in there as if they were journal entries."
>
> Ntozake Shange

> "I put things down on sheets of paper and stuff them in my pockets. When I have enough, I have a book."
>
> John Lennon

Writing Down the Days: 365 Creative Journaling Ideas for Young People by Lorraine M. Dahlstrom (Minneapolis: Free Spirit Publishing Inc., 1990). This book has a year's worth of writing exercises that encourage creativity and self-discovery.

 **Write Now...**

Once you choose a journal and pen you like, make your first entry a letter to yourself. Write about everything you want to record in your journal and why. Make a lavish list of every possible topic that interests you. This is your personal "table of contents" (not in any order) of what you might write about. You can refer back to this page whenever you need inspiration and add to it as new ideas pop into your head.

> "*The Catcher in the Rye* was a door-opener for me. It made me see that adolescence could be something very dramatic to write about."
>
> Robert Cormier

Here's everything I want to write about:

- When my grandfather had a heart attack and died.
- Traveling in the subways of London.
- The first time I went on the largest roller coaster in the world.
- The first time someone really kissed me and I kissed back.
- Stories my grandmother told me about Finland.
- My dream car.
- Sailing.
- Getting lost in Chicago when I was thirteen.
- A murder mystery where my dog solves the crime.

John, 16

And remember, when it comes to journal writing, don't worry about staying on the straight-and-narrow path. Feel free to wander, wonder, sketch, stretch, rant, rave, drift, doodle, imagine, and write nonsense. Let your journal writing go anywhere you please.

Start Your Own Library

You may have heard that it's important to read other writers so you can get ideas, find a style you love, and learn how to polish your own writing and your command of the language. This is true. Reading other writers does all of this and more.

Writers often have a personal library stocked with their favorite books by their favorite authors. To start your own library, visit used or half-price bookstores, regular bookstores, or garage sales to see what's available, affordable, and interesting to you. Other books that might prove helpful are collections of inspiring quotes, a dictionary, a thesaurus, an atlas, or any other resources that can spur your own words.

Read anything that interests you—novels, short stories, essays, nonfiction, poems, biographies, children's books, young-adult fiction, journals of famous people, newspapers, and magazines. Read the work of writers who lived in fancy sixteenth-century courts and wrote endless sonnets about dying roses. Or writers who live on the prairie and write about hawks, tractors, and lukewarm coffee. Or punk writers who hang out in a small café in Budapest. Read song lyrics, zines, comic novels, literary magazines, or whatever catches your interest.

Read. Read. Read.

When you read the works of other writers, you join the community of people who love books, stories, poems, essays, plays, and other forms of writing. You share with them the intense feelings of wonder and pleasure that words written on a piece of paper or bound in a book may spark. Joining the global community of readers and writers can help you feel more connected to sources of inspiration and encouragement.

> "Read a lot and hit the streets. A writer who doesn't keep up with what's out there ain't gonna be out there."
>
> Toni Cade Bambara

 **Write Now...**

Make a list of all the writers—dead or living, male or female, from this country or anywhere else in the world—you want to read. If you need ideas, ask people you admire (your parents, relatives, teachers, friends) about whose works they like to read and why. See if you can find a new writer to explore. Then head to your local library or bookstore to find books by and about the writers you've chosen. Dive in!

You can create a page in your journal to keep track of the books you've read. Also jot down any favorite lines or passages; these can serve as references for your own writing.

 WRITER'S CORNER

Walking on Alligators: A Book of Meditations for Writers by Susan Shaughnessy (San Francisco: Harper San Francisco, 1993). This is a book full of inspiring quotes from inspiring writers—a good thing to have on the shelf.

Pick Your Genre

Genre? (Pronounced zhjon´-ra.) A French word . . . cultured, spelled and pronounced strangely, and tossed around in art and literature classes like dough in a pizza parlor. Genre basically refers to the category of writing (or art) you've chosen. Plays, poetry, fiction, and nonfiction are examples of literary genres. Each one has its own style, form, and content.

You'll also find genres within genres. For example, African-American women's novels are a genre within the genre of the "novel," which is a genre within the genre of "fiction." (Note: Fiction refers to imaginary stories; the opposite of this is non-fiction, or literature based on truth.)

Genres are similar to the animal classifications (mammals, reptiles, birds, fish, and so on) you might have studied in science class. You can tell which group an animal fits into by identifying its main physical characteristics—lungs, gills, fur, scales, feathers. In much the same way, you can identify a form of writing by its makeup. For example, if the written work is fairly short and rhymes, it's probably a poem. If the writing contains lines like this . . .

Curtain rises to reveal a dark stage. We hear the sounds of two people entering a room.

THIEF. (whispering) Be quiet.

ACCOMPLICE. (whispering) You be quiet. (pause) I'm scared. What if we get caught?

. . . it's probably a play.

Sometimes it's not so simple to identify what category a piece of writing fits into. This is because writers often borrow techniques from a variety of genres to create a unique style of their own. Have you read the Winnie-the-Pooh books by A. A. Milne? An English poet and playwright, Milne often included poetry or verse in his Pooh stories. Shakespeare, too, incorporated poems and songs into his plays. Poet and fiction writer Sandra Cisneros blended genres in her book *The House on Mango Street,* which tells the story of a young girl named Esperanza through a series of mini-chapters that read almost like poetry.

As a writer, you should feel free to write in any genre, to move from one genre to the next, and to mix genres (include poetry in your bone-chilling mystery about a werewolf, if you want). If you decide to write about a woman who takes care of hundreds of cats, you could create a play, a narrative poem (a poem that tells a story), a short story, a novel, or even an essay (if the information is true). Choose genres that seem to call to you or that you want to experiment with. If one genre doesn't feel right, try another.

Following is a starter list of genres:

• **Poetry:** A poem usually conveys a vivid and imaginative sense of experience, perception, meaning, or emotion. Poetry uses as few words as possible, and each word is chosen for how

"Why are we reading, if not in hope of beauty laid bare, life heightened and its deepest mystery probed?"

Annie Dillard

it sounds as well as what it says. Because poetry focuses so much on rhythm and sound, it's a form of writing that falls somewhere between music and prose—a poem may be read aloud for the pleasure of how it sounds, and may or may not rhyme.

- **Novel:** A novel is a long story (short novels are called *novellas*). According to the *American Heritage Dictionary,* a novel usually has "a plot that is unfolded by the actions, speech, and thoughts of the characters." *Plot* refers to what happens in the story. In addition to plot, novels usually contain a *theme* (an overall meaning), a *setting* (the place and time in which the story happens), *tone* (the mood of the story), *characterizations* (developed characters), and *dialogue* (what the characters say). For further explanation of these terms, see "Know Your Terms" on pages 44–45.

- **Short story:** A short story can be just a few pages or nearly as long as a novella, but the narrative usually focuses on *mood* (what the reader and the characters feel) rather than *plot* (what happens). Like novels, short stories often include a theme, setting, tone, characterizations, and dialogue. Because short stories are shorter, every word counts. There are also short short stories, which are *really* short, usually under five hundred words and sometimes just a paragraph.

- **Play:** A play is a literary work written for the stage or screen. Plays are dramatized, or performed, so the focus is mainly on dialogue. Dialogue reveals what the characters feel and who they truly are. In a play, the setting is created through the use of the stage set, *backdrop* (a painted cloth hung at the rear of the stage), props, and the actors' costumes. Stage directions need to be provided for the actors, so they know where to go, what to say, and how to act.

- **Essay:** In an essay, the writer discusses a subject using a personal point of view. An essay can be about anything from mosquitoes to plumbing to the vanishing ozone layer. Essays often attempt to persuade the reader to accept the writer's point of view.

- **Literary nonfiction and creative nonfiction:** These works describe true events in a storylike way. The focus is on telling the "story" of the event, describing the setting (the place where the event took place), and developing the characters (the people involved). Other types of nonfiction include biographies, autobiographies, how-to books or articles, journals, and any other works that are based on truth.

- **Science fiction, fantasy, and horror:** Science fiction writing explores actual or potential scientific discoveries and developments. The characters often include extraterrestrials (beings that reside or originate outside of Earth). Fantasy writing focuses on supernatural or fanciful elements like dragons, mermaids, unicorns, enchanted forests, and otherworldly beings and places. Horror writing uses vampires, monsters, ghosts, and other scary subjects. Science fiction, fantasy, and horror usually appear in the form of a novel or short story, but it's also possible for them to be poems or plays.

- **Mystery:** A mystery is a story that involves a puzzling crime or other mystifying situation. Mysteries may be presented as novels, short stories, or plays. Usually they're written so that readers can follow the clues and figure out, or be surprised by, the ending.

Did You Know?

In 1931, China banned Lewis Carroll's *Alice's Adventures in Wonderland* because officials believed that animals shouldn't use human language or be put on the same level as people.

 WRITER'S CORNER

How to Write a Story by Kathleen C. Phillips (New York: Franklin Watts, 1995). The author shows how to develop characters, build plots, create settings, and write captivating dialogue.

How to Write Tales of Horror, Fantasy and Science Fiction by J. N. Williamson (Cincinnati, OH: Writer's Digest Books, 1991). This book is a good, very readable guide to these genres.

Poem-Making by Myra Cohn Livingston (New York: HarperCollins, 1991). This lively book covers many types of poems, poetic forms, and figures of speech. It also includes writing exercises.

Writing Fiction: A Guide to Narrative Craft by Janet Burroway (Reading, MA: Addison Wesley Longman Inc., 1995). This is a reader-friendly guide to putting together stories and novels.

Know Your Terms

When people talk about the craft of writing, a bunch of words get thrown around. If you understand these words, you may find it easier to speak more clearly about your own writing. (As a bonus, knowing these terms will give you an edge in discussing and writing about literature in your English classes.)

Following is a list of literary terms you'll want to get familiar with:

- **Plot:** Plot is what happens in a story or play—the sequence of action and events that occur. For example, the plot of *Romeo and Juliet* is boy meets girl, boy loses girl, boy gets girl back, boy thinks girl dies, boy kills himself, girl kills herself.

- **Theme:** Theme is the underlying message of a piece of writing. It answers the question "What is this work about?" Themes—love conquers all, man or woman against nature, survival of the human spirit—tell us about the world in some way.

- **Setting:** The setting of a story or another piece of work refers to the time and place where everything happens. For example, the setting of *Lord of the Flies* by William Golding is a deserted tropical island where a group of English schoolboys are stranded after a plane wreck.

- **Scene:** Scene includes the setting (time and place) as well as the people involved and the events taking place. The term is also used by playwrights: plays are usually divided into acts (kind of like big chapters), and the acts are then divided into scenes, or little subdivisions in which the action occurs.

- **Imagery:** Imagery is a picture of something you paint with your words, usually appealing to one or more of the senses: sight, taste, touch, hearing, and smell. For example, "The runaway boy hid beneath a discarded cardboard box as rain pounded the city streets." Can you hear the torrents of rain? Can you feel the water slapping the box and smell the soggy cardboard?

Did You Know?

The Catcher in the Rye by J. D. Salinger is the book most frequently banned by the American school system.

- **Point of view:** This refers to the perspective of who's telling the story. The perspective can be first person (I, me, myself), third person (he, she, they), or second person (you, yours). *Voice* describes the general mood of the speaker. *Tone* expresses the attitude of the author or the mood of the writing, which might be ironic, angry, humorous, or sarcastic, for example.

- **Characters:** Characters, very simply, are the people or creatures in your writing. The way you reveal their personalities—through descriptions of their voices, gestures, actions, words, and how other characters respond to them—is *characterization* You can get a feel for characterization by thinking about what your characters like, dislike, need, say, dream, feel, and fear.

- **Dialogue:** Dialogue is basically what the characters in your writing say. Plays rely heavily on dialogue to help express what the characters are feeling and doing. Poems, on the other hand, usually don't use much dialogue.

You may find it helpful to copy these definitions into your journal so you can refer to them when you're writing.

As you write stories, poems, plays, or other forms of literature, ask yourself if you've incorporated the basic elements of the genre you've chosen. For example, does your story have a theme? Does your poem include vivid imagery? Is your essay persuasive? Is your play filled with relevant dialogue? Have you maintained a consistent tone in your writing? Are your characters realistic, authentic, or interesting, and will your reader care about them? Does the plot of your story make sense and follow a logical sequence? Is your setting imaginative? Have you taken care to develop each scene and to make each one flow into the next? Is there anything you can do to make your writing stronger, more purposeful, more *believable?*

> "When you're writing, you're operating out of some different part of the brain. When it's happening, you're not aware of it, you don't know where what you write is coming from. And when you read it later, you think, Wow. I did that? It's like a surprise."
>
> Judy Blume

Use Your Tools

Becoming a writer happens slowly over time. You start thinking that you'd like to write, you write a little, and you want to write more. Maybe after a few months or years, you start to think of yourself as someone who likes to write. Maybe you eventually begin to think of yourself as a writer.

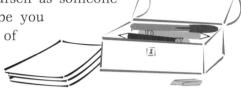

Meanwhile, you fill up diaries and journals, scratch paper and index cards, computer disks and notebooks. You witness things happening or feel strong emotions, and immediately you start translating these experiences into the written word—*your* written word. Eventually, you read over something you've written, and you recognize the voice as your own. And you start to know yourself through this voice.

But all of this takes time.

Becoming a writer is a *process*. It's not as if you wake up one day, decide to be a writer, and—presto!—write a best-selling novel. Instead, you may spend years building your skills as a writer. And to build, you need to make good use of your tools. Here are some skill-building tips to try:

1. Be descriptive. Describe your characters and images in ways your reader will understand—and be sure to avoid confusing references and boring details. For example, if you're describing the burrito your character just made and you say it's as hot and spicy as one your dad made for you when you were nine, your reader probably won't be able to relate to what you're saying. To be descriptive and original, you might write that the burrito was "spicy enough to make your eyes water just looking at it."

Read books, poems, plays, and other forms of writing to see how published writers use description in their works. Are there any descriptions that stand out in your mind? Copy them in your journal, so you can refer to them whenever you need ideas for developing your own technique.

> "Description needs to slide into a story like a snake through grass— silently, almost invisibly, without calling attention to itself."
>
> Marion Dane Bauer

Write Now...

To practice your skills, pick an object and list as many words as you can think of that would describe it to someone who can't see it. What color is it? Is it big or small? Round or edgy? Can people sit, stand, sleep, or jump on it? Is it used for decoration? Does the object have a smell or particular type of surface? Is it alive? How might the object make someone feel?

Once you've exhausted all the possible details, circle the ones on your list that you think are the most important or best describe your object. Next, write a paragraph describing your object without ever naming it. When you're finished, give your paragraph to some friends and see if they can figure out what you're describing. What details could you have added to make it easier for your friends to guess your object? What details could you have left out?

Try this exercise again and again, describing a new object each time. Soon, it should get easier to choose the most important and interesting details.

2. Show, don't tell. Details can hold whole lives in them. Even small or seemingly unimportant snippets of information—a desk full of papers, dirt underneath fingernails, a pair of too-tight shoes—can tell a reader worlds about the characters, the tone, and the theme of your work.

Learn to be descriptive and to present interesting details without *telling* your reader, in so many words, exactly what you're trying to convey. For example, a description like the following doesn't leave much to the reader's imagination: "Alisha nervously waited on stage for the announcer to read the first-place winner. When he finally read her name, she was so excited to have won first place!"

But something like this . . .

The audience watched in anticipation as the announcer fumbled with the envelope containing the winner's name. Alisha's heart raced, and her palms began to sweat.

"All the fun's in how you say a thing."

Robert Frost

Did You Know?

The 1991 novel *Gadsby* by Ernest Vincent Wright has 267 pages, about 50,000 words, and doesn't use the letter *E*. The author purposely challenged himself with the puzzle of not using *E*, one of the most common letters of the alphabet.

As the announcer pulled the card out of the envelope, Alisha tilted her head back and looked toward the bright lights beaming down on the contestants. "Please, please, please," she mouthed.

. . . allows your readers to *feel* firsthand the tension and excitement of the situation.

3. Create vivid settings. Have you ever read Harper Lee's classic novel, *To Kill a Mockingbird*? The author's portrayal of small-town Alabama in the 1930s is so authentic, you can't help but be drawn into the mysteries and conflicts of the people who populate it. As you read the story, you can almost feel the summer heat, smell the magnolia trees, hear the characters' distinct rhythms of speech, and sense the violence that's about to erupt. When you create vivid and imaginative settings like this, readers are naturally more interested and involved.

Suppose you're writing a mystery and you want to describe a ghost in the attic of a creepy Victorian house. Your reader might be bored to tears reading this: "It was 1846. The tall house was creepy in the dark. A ghost appeared in the attic, scaring the family to death."

On the other hand, a description like this . . .

Mrs. Adams sat in the parlor, the gentle folds of her skirt brushing the floor. Her children sat quietly, listening to the bedtime story she read by the light of an oil lamp. As she turned the page, an eerily familiar noise sounded from above: the creaking of attic floorboards followed by a scream. The lamp's flame winked out, and the family was left in darkness.

. . . might capture your reader's attention.

You can use vivid settings in nonfiction writing as well. Suppose you're writing an essay about endangered prairie dogs. Instead of saying something like "Today, prairie dogs are an endangered animal," you could start out your essay with the following scene:

> "I try to leave out the parts that people skip."
>
> Elmore Leonard

> "The right word may be effective, but no word was ever as effective as a rightly timed pause."
>
> Mark Twain

On a recent spring morning in Colorado, hundreds of prairie dogs popped their heads in and out of the ground, one after another. A light breeze carried the lively sounds of their chirping. Without warning a truck pulled up. On its side were the words "Pest Control."

An opening like this gives the reader a stronger visual picture of what you're communicating and lends a sense of urgency to your message.

Whether you write fiction or nonfiction, just be careful not to get so carried away describing the setting that your reader almost needs a map to find his or her way around. Your reader may lose track of the action and quit reading. How many times have you skipped over long descriptions of forest and sky (the pattern of branches, the darkening clouds) to finally get to the part where the dragon swoops down? Remember to keep the heart of the poem, story, essay, or play beating loud enough so your reader can hear it.

 **Write Now...**

To practice setting the scene, start with somewhere familiar—maybe your room at home, a favorite park, the cafeteria at school. Describe the surroundings on an ordinary day. What do you see as you look around? What are people doing? What's the general mood? What makes this a typical day? Give enough details that a reader can imagine being in the scene. What does the reader see and feel while walking around?

Now take your place and move it to another location. For example, if your place was the school cafeteria, what would it look like if it was in Quito, Ecuador? How would this day differ from a day at your own school cafeteria?

Or, instead of moving your place to a new location, try changing the circumstances. For example, if you wrote about an ordinary day at the park, write about an *extraordinary* day there. Maybe your town is experiencing the hottest, driest summer on record. Maybe the river that flows through the park has flooded part of the town. What would this scene look like? How would

"Stories have a richness that goes way beyond fact. My writing knows more than I know. What a writer must do is listen to her book. It might take you where you don't expect to go."

Madeleine L'Engle

things be different under these circumstances? How does the mood differ from before?

Practice setting the scene from time to time, and see how you can change what your reader sees and feels. Save these descriptions for when you need new ideas or locations in your writing.

 WRITER'S CORNER

Our Stories: A Fiction Workshop for Young Authors by Marion Dane Bauer (New York: Clarion, 1996). In this book, young authors learn how to refine their fiction-writing techniques—develop characters, create effective dialogue, establish point of view—by examining thirty selections written by students in grades 4–12. Bauer critiques each writing sample and suggests ways to make the writing stronger.

4. Find a rhythm. Creative writing stands somewhere between music and painting, sight and sound. It's visual, but it's also *aural* (meaning that you hear it). The collective *rhythm* of your writing can say as much to your reader as your choice of individual words.

The sound of a word can be just as important as its literal meaning. Some sounds are hard *(task, crunch, crack)*, while others are soft *(lamb, moon, leaf)*. Each sentence or paragraph speaks to your reader through its rhythm. You can write in a rhythm that matches your theme, or you can write in a rhythm that contrasts your theme, depending on the effect you want.

For example, if you're writing a murder scene, you might choose words that sound harsh and evoke images of darkness, suspense, and death *(crash, blasted, accused)*. If you're describing a dream where you were able to fly through the clouds, you might choose softer, lighter words *(free, melody, blue)*.

The balance between silence and sound also affects the rhythm of your writing. If, for example, a poem has a lot of open space, short lines, pauses, and gaps, it's using silence to help communicate its message. Stories and plays can do the same thing through changing the length of sentences and paragraphs. Pauses, word use, and rhythm—they all add up to create the *sound* of what you write.

> "One has to work very carefully with what is in between the words. What is not said. Which is measure, which is rhythm and so on. So, it is what you don't write that frequently gives what you do write its power."
>
> Toni Morrison

One of the best ways to improve your writing is to read it aloud, either alone or to others. Listen to find out whether your words speed up during action scenes, become playful during funny scenes, or slow down during lazy scenes. Reading your work out loud will help point out clumsy sentences, an awkward rhythm, or writing that just doesn't make sense.

One thing you might consider adding to your writer's library is your favorite book on tape. You can learn a lot about the sound of writing when you hear a story unfold word by word.

"Read your work aloud! This is the best advice I can give. When you read aloud you find out how much can be cut, how much is unnecessary. You hear how the story flows. And nothing teaches you as much about writing dialogue as listening to it."

Judy Blume

PART 2

Diving into Your Life: Making Waves of Your Own

"I can't remember a time when I wasn't trying to get something down on paper. . . . I can't remember a time, really, when I haven't been a writer. That was always my escape, you know; reading and writing. Those were the two great escapes of my life and I suppose they still are."
ROBERT CORMIER

Ever wonder where writers get their ideas? Maybe you read a story and think, "I wish I could come up with an idea like that!"

So where *do* they get their ideas?

Pulitzer Prize-winner and former Poet Laureate Rita Dove was riding on a bus in Williamsburg, Virginia, when her teenage daughter nudged her and whispered, "Hey, we're on the bus with Rosa Parks!" Sure enough, Parks was sitting in one of the front bus seats. This inspired some of the poems in Dove's collection of poetry titled *On the Bus with Rosa Parks*. When author Robert Cormier's son refused to sell chocolates during his school's annual sale as a statement of principle (but with his parents' permission), *The Chocolate War* was born. And young-adult fiction writer Chris Crutcher says the idea for his novel *Running Loose* came from a conversation he overheard in a locker room about a racist coach who encouraged his players to eliminate a black player. Ideas can come from *anywhere* at any time.

All writers, though, experience a period when ideas aren't flowing. (Award-winning novelist M. E. Kerr describes this as feeling like the words "NO IDEA" are written across your forehead.) Most authors agree that ideas can't be forced—they come when they're ready, and you can't always anticipate what will set them in motion. But you *can* be ready when they finally arrive!

CHAPTER 4

Discovering Your World

Sources of ideas are all around you, so look and be ready to grab them. Photographs, songs, quotes, conversations, funny experiences, hard times: everything is fair game in your writing. Use your world—what you see, how you feel, what you wish for—as inspiration for your writing. Keep your eyes open, and your pen will start moving across the page.

When you look at the world around you, what do you see? Most likely, everyday things like cars, buildings, people, streets, trees, buses, animals, and so on. No big deal, right? But look closer. Maybe the old man you see waiting at the bus stop each day has the ability to read people's minds, or has a hundred great-grandchildren, or is the king of a small island he owns off the coast of Hawaii. Who knows?

People, objects, nature, music—all of these things, when experienced through the eyes of a writer, can be a rich source of inspiration. With a little practice and a lot of imagination, you can see the extraordinary in the ordinary.

Did You Know?

Author Truman Capote was the model used for the young character Dill in Harper Lee's *To Kill a Mockingbird.* Capote and Lee were childhood friends.

Tell Your Tale

Do you remember the first fairy tale or myth you ever read or listened to? Was it one of the Grimm Brothers' original tales like *Cinderella* or *Snow White*? Was it *The Eagles of Lost Opportunity* (North America, Delaware Indian), *The Wonderful Pear Tree* (China), or *Why Cat and Rat Are No Longer Friends* (Central

Africa)? Do you remember how the tale affected you and what you learned from it?

In many cultures, fairy tales and myths are more than just entertaining stories: they teach a society's deeply held values and beliefs. For example, Native American myths like *The Woman Who Fell from the Sky: The Iroquois Story of Creation* serve to explain how the world was created, why the seasons change, how humans came into being, and how animals acquired certain characteristics. Fairy tales and myths from all parts of the world teach the difference between right and wrong, fair and unfair, good and evil (kind-hearted Cinderella wins the heart of the prince, while the evil stepsisters look on with envy; the Beast turns back into a handsome prince after he earns the love of Beauty). Such fairy tales teach that good behavior is almost always rewarded by the chance to live "happily ever after."

Writers of every genre have used fairy tales and myths as the inspiration for their stories, poems, plays, and movies. For example, screenwriter and director George Lucas says he wrote the *Star Wars* trilogy with mythology in mind. *Star Wars* is a classic example of good versus evil. The tale of Darth Vader, Luke Skywalker, and the "Force" explores how and why one person chooses to remain good, while another is tempted and overtaken by the "Dark Side."

As for your own writing, feel free to use the characters, plots, themes, and settings from the world's gigantic library of myths and tales as the basis for your own creations. Think of writing from tales as a way to explore what great myths *you* believe—being swept off your feet in love, good prevailing over evil, living happily ever after—and how these stories influence the way you view the world.

> "Deeper meaning resides in the fairy tales told to me in my childhood than in the truth that is taught by life."
>
> Friedrich Schiller

 WRITER'S CORNER

African Myths and Legends by Kathleen Arnott (New York: Oxford University Press, 1990). Collected from all parts of Africa, the stories in this book include magical drums, flying horses, and greedy spiders.

American Indian Myths and Legends edited by Richard Erdoes and Alfonso Ortiz (New York: Pantheon Books, 1985). One hundred sixty tales from eighty tribal groups offer a glimpse into Native American mystic heritage.

The Classic Fairy Tales edited by Iona and Peter Opie (New York: Oxford University Press, 1983). This book presents the texts of twenty-four well-known fairy tales as they were first presented in English and summarizes the history of each tale.

Folktales from India: A Selection of Oral Tales from Twenty-Two Languages by A. K. Ramamujan (New York: Pantheon Books, 1994). This is a collection of 110 tales translated from twenty-two languages from India's folklore tradition.

The Rain Forest Storybook: Traditional Stories from the Original Forest Peoples of South America, Africa, and South-East Asia by Rosalind Kerven (New York: Cambridge University Press, 1994). This is a collection of folktales from various people living in rain forests around the world.

Tales of Wonder
http://darsie.ucdavis.edu/tales/
This Web site contains folk and fairy tales from around the world, including Russia, China, the Middle East, and Ireland. It also includes links to other fairy tale sites.

Write Now...

Select a book of myths or fairy tales. Without looking at the index or table of contents, randomly open the book to a story. Allow fate to pick out the tale that will launch you into your own story, poem, essay, or other form of writing. Read the tale, and then pick one of the following ideas for your own writing:

- Become one of the characters in the tale and tell his or her side of the story (what "really" happened). For instance, you might write a story from Bluebeard's perspective, explaining how he (you) got a "bad rap." Or you might be Cinderella's step-mother and write about what it was like to live with goody-goody Cinderella.

- Set the scene of the tale in your present-day life, substituting your family and friends for the characters in the fairy tale. For example, the setting of *The Little Mermaid* could be your school. Pretend the school is the underwater community ruled by the Sea King (the principal), and life outside is the world of humans.

"We remember wonder tales and fairy tales to keep our sense of wonderment alive and to nurture our hope that we can seize possibilities and opportunities to transform ourselves and our worlds."

Jack Zipes

- Write beyond the end of the story—what happens after the last line you read? For example, what happens after they live "happily ever after"? Does Snow White grow bored with Prince Charming? Do the dwarves begin selling real estate in the forest?

```
Everyone gives me a bad name, like it was my
fault she washed the floor. What they don't know
is that she needed to wash things. Cinderella had
obsessive-compulsive disorder, and cleaning
chimneys was part of her therapy. She was also
very shy, so shy that dances terrified her. So I
let her stay home and sleep on the sofa where she
felt safe. I even gave her my oldest, warmest
blanket because she loved that one best.
    What people don't know is that she never did go
to the ball. The glass slipper fit her. Yes, that
happened, but that's just because she has small
feet and so did that mysterious princess. You know,
many women wear the same shoe size.
    If you don't believe me, go to the castle right
now. You'll find her there all right, on the floor
in the kitchen, scrubbing. The king hired a whole
carriage of therapists but none of them do any good.
As for me, I just miss her warm smile and wish she
could be back with me who understands her best.
                                        Laura, 15
```

> "Don't ever hesitate to imitate another writer—every artist learning his craft needs some models. Eventually you will find your own voice and shed the skin of the writer you imitated."
>
> William Zinsser

Write from the Story

"Now that the fear has been rummaged down to the husk," wrote Galway Kinnell in his poem "The Still Time." From that line, I was inspired to write a long poem about looking deeply into something I feared until the fear was just a bare shell of itself.

When I sat down to write that day, I hadn't planned to write about something I feared. But something about Kinnell's line propelled me in that direction. You, too, can use someone's words to encourage your own.

Starting from someone else's writing takes the pressure off to do what many writers consider the hardest task of all: writing the first line. A good first line is important—it's what helps your reader decide whether to continue reading. It sets the tone for the rest of your writing and can be the most memorable line of all. (Ever heard "Call me Ishmael" before? Or what about "It was the best of times, it was the worst of times"? These famous openers are from *Moby Dick* and *A Tale of Two Cities*.)

Good first lines draw in your reader—they make your reader want to know more. Alice Walker begins her Pulitzer Prize-winning novel *The Color Purple* like this (she uses italics for emphasis): *"You better not never tell nobody but God. It'd kill your mammy."* You know right away something terrible has happened—so terrible it shouldn't be spoken aloud. What reader wouldn't be compelled to find out what it was?

Skim through some of your favorite stories or poems and find an opening line (or any line) that catches your eye. Use this as your first line and idea-starter. How many different story ideas can you develop from the same first line? Could you write a poem, a comedy, a horror piece, and a work of science fiction using the same beginning? Does the rest of your writing flow more easily without the pressure of coming up with a great first line?

Here are some starting line suggestions:

My mother had two faces and a frying pot
"From the House of Yemanjá" by Audre Lorde

Droning a drowsy syncopated tune,
"The Weary Blues" by Langston Hughes

i am accused of tending to the past
"i am accused of tending to the past" by Lucille Clifton

Now, I don't like school, which you might say is one of the factors that got us involved with this old guy we nicknamed The Pigman.
The Pigman by Paul Zindel

"What's so hard about the first sentence is that you're stuck with it. Everything else is going to flow out of that sentence."

Joan Didion

Did You Know?

S. Porter, who wrote using the name O. Henry, started his writing career in prison, where he spent three years after being convicted for embezzlement when he worked as a bank teller.

60

When I stepped out into the bright sunlight from the darkness of the movie house, I had only two things on my mind.
The Outsiders by S. E. Hinton

Ships at a distance have every man's wish on board.
Their Eyes Were Watching God by Zora Neale Hurston

Just for fun, flip through *It Was a Dark and Stormy Night: The Best (?) from the Bulwer-Lytton Contest* compiled by Scott Rice (see "Writer's Corner" below). Every year, San Jose State University's English department sponsors the Bulwer-Lytton Fiction Contest, which challenges people to enter their *worst* opening lines. The "best" entries have been compiled in the series of books. For example, "The rains splattered down on the tables of the cafe like raisins dropped by uncaring gods," or "The horizon coughed up the morning sun much as if Atlas had lowered the world from his mighty shoulders and given it the Heimlich maneuver." You may never use any of these lines as your opener, but they might inspire ideas (or a laugh)!

 **WRITER'S CORNER**

The First Line
P.O. Box 0382
Plano, TX 75025-0382
http://thefirstline.com/
This literary magazine, a publication of K Street Ink, contains stories all written from the same first line. Each issue contains the best submitted stories created from a shared opening line chosen by the editors. Check out the Web site or the latest edition to find out the opening line for the next issue and submission deadlines.

It Was a Dark and Stormy Night: The Best (?) from the Bulwer-Lytton Contest compiled by Scott Rice (New York: Penguin, 1984). Entertain yourself by reading selections taken from the Bulwer-Lytton Fiction Contest for the best of bad fiction. The world-famous competition seeks to find the most atrocious opening sentence to a hypothetical lousy novel.

> "Writing the opening lines of a story is a bit like starting to ski at the steepest part of a hill. You must have all your skills under control from the first instant."
>
> Marion Dane Bauer

Rhythmic Repetitions

Writing, like music, can use the technique of rhythm and repetition to influence the reader or listener. A good example of this is Joy Harjo's poem "She Had Some Horses," in which the poet, who's a member of the Creek Indian tribe, repeats the phrase "She had horses" at the beginning of each sentence. This repetition creates a chantlike rhythm designed to mesmerize the reader: "She had horses who were bodies of sand. / She had horses who were maps drawn of blood." The poem continues, but already you can hear the arrangement of the rhythm: it sounds like a herd of wild horses thundering across a field.

Word repetition can produce a state of deep relaxation, almost like a trance (so it's no wonder many prayers in many religions repeat phrases). In a state of relaxation, people may rejoice and feel a greater sense of unity or belonging. The right phrase can unlock feelings hidden deep inside. Let these deeper emotions guide your writing.

Many scholars and music lovers believe that music, like word repetition, has the power to heal, soothe, and transform your emotions. As with a certain phrase, music can give rise to all kinds of feelings and memories. As the "soundtrack" to your life, music can take you back to events, places, and people who were with you when a particular song was playing—your first kiss, your best vacation, your first time behind the wheel of a car. And similar to repetition, music has the ability to relax you and open your mind to new ideas.

By writing to music, you can absorb its magic into your words. Feel free to experiment with different types of music to find what works best for you. Maybe it's the score to *Rent* that makes you most productive, or maybe it's Beethoven, the Smashing Pumpkins, Garth Brooks, or the Gipsy Kings. When you change the music's tempo—from Mozart to Latin music, for example—you can alter the tone and rhythm of your writing.

> "Music is another way of thinking, or maybe thinking is another kind of music."
>
> Ursula K. Le Guin

62

"Music is the vernacular of the human soul."

Geoffrey Latham

Here's a list of musicians from different cultures you might want to explore:

- Bulgarian Women's Choir
  (Bulgarian and other Slavic music)

- The Chieftains (Irish music)

- R. Carlos Nakai (Native American flute)

- Ravi Shankar (sitar music from India)

- Ladysmith Black Mambazo
  (African choral music)

- Juan Luis Guerra (Latin music)

- Kodo (Japanese Taiko drumming)

- Papa Wemba (African pop music)

 **Write Now...**

Let the rhythm of music lead you deeper into your writing. Begin by listening to music and freewriting on any topic for at least ten minutes. Write whatever comes to mind. See if the style of music influences what you write.

Review what you wrote, and pick out a phrase that evokes some response in you. If you can't find a phrase that speaks to you, use "She (or He) had some (fill in the blank)" and run with it.

Begin a poem or story with this phrase and write wherever it leads you. When you get to the end of that idea or image, write the phrase over again, and see where your writing goes this time. If you change the style of music, do any new thoughts come to mind?

Take a break, and later read aloud what you wrote. Listen for the rhythm in your writing. How far did the music take you?

```
Soon the land becomes lower
As the wagon train moves toward Texas
And the sky becomes dark as the storm rumbles
Soon the land becomes lower.

Soon the land becomes lower
As the soldiers marched on
To stop and set up camp
As the storm approaches.
Soon the land becomes lower.
                              Steph, 13
```

Write About the Ordinary

Hold the peach, try the weight, sweetness
and death so round and snug
in your palm.
And, so, there is
the weight of memory . . .

In this poem, "The Weight of Sweetness," the poet Li-Young Lee, while writing about something as ordinary as a peach, is able to slide his way into writing about death and "the weight of memory." He finds a path from the peach to a story about his father and himself as a boy—a story that shows how bittersweet some memories can be. An extraordinary poem . . . and it all starts with something as ordinary as a peach.

Food is something that just about any writer—and reader—can relate to. The smell of baking bread, the sizzle and snap of frying sausages, the salty-sweet taste of buttered sweetcorn in summer are images familiar to most readers. Yet, these common scents, sounds, and tastes could suggest different meanings depending on how you use them. For example, the sound of sausages frying in the pan might recall happy Saturday mornings when the whole family gathered for a hearty breakfast. On the other hand, it could suggest suffering over a hot stove, getting spattered by sizzling grease. Either way, the image produces an emotional response.

Food can tell tales about your characters and how they relate to each other. In Amy Tan's novel *The Joy Luck Club,* for instance, a passage reads: "As is the Chinese cook's custom, my mother always made disparaging remarks about her own cooking. That night she chose to direct it toward her famous steamed pork and preserved vegetable dish, which she always served with special pride. 'Ai! This dish not salty enough, no flavor,' she complained, after tasting a small bite. 'It is too bad to eat.' This was our family's cue to eat some and proclaim it the best she had ever made." Food is universal, yet personal. You can use it in your writing to add depth and dimension to certain characters and scenes.

Just make sure you choose your images carefully. Something like this . . .

My dad carried the salad consisting of lettuce, tomatoes, cucumbers, and croutons to the table. He set it down by the spaghetti with marinara sauce, then passed around some whole wheat rolls.

. . . doesn't tell your reader much more than that your family enjoys a well-balanced meal.

On the other hand, something like this . . .

A mound of spaghetti in red sauce sat in a bowl right in the center of the table. Dad, still wearing his apron, beamed at it. The rest of us stared at the heaping bowl, hoping someone else would have the courage to take the first helping. No one had the heart to tell him that his "secret sauce" usually tasted like burnt ketchup.

. . . gives your reader an amusing insight into your dad and the rest of your family.

Like a favorite song, food can be an emotional springboard for your writing. It's something personal and yet, at the same time, everyone can relate to it. See what happens when you explore ordinary, everyday things like food in your writing. Can it reveal anything about you, your family, your friends, or your life?

Write Now...

Take a moment to imagine what would make the greatest meal ever. If you could choose anyone, past or present, to join you, who would it be? Your entire family? Your favorite movie star? Or would you prefer to dine alone? Where would the meal be served—on a blanket in the moonlight on an abandoned tropical island or in the middle of your grandmother's tiny apartment with tons of children running around? How many courses would your meal have?

Close your eyes and imagine the place, company, food, plates, utensils, tablecloths, and furniture. Then start writing, describing in detail why this is the greatest meal of your life. Here are some ideas you can use:

Did You Know?

Gertrude Stein often wrote in her car, which she named "Godiva." She believed that sitting in the driver's seat, while parked curbside, was an inspiring place to write.

- How is the food prepared and presented?

- What does it taste like?

- Who prepared the food?

- What are you and your guests wearing?

- How is the setting lit—with sunlight, candles, lamps?

- Is this meal for a special occasion—your birthday, a movie premiere, a huge family reunion?

- How do you eat the meal—slowly, quickly, with chopsticks?

- Don't forget dessert!

He carries the basket ahead of me and turns to smile. I smile back. We are walking across sand dunes on a quiet and empty beach somewhere in North Carolina. It's just sunrise, and the sky is filled with dark purple and gray and fiery red light all over the clouds.

Soon he stops. I spread a soft purple blanket, and we sit down. He opens the basket and lifts out, one by one, our delicious breakfast: orange marmalade, a stack of hot and crispy bacon, warm French toast stuffed with apricot cream cheese, real maple syrup, honeydew melon, sparkling grape spritzer, and a thermos of hazelnut decaf lattes. I lift out the blue-and-white china with pictures of Chinese pagodas on them, two peach-colored mugs, and two wine glasses for the soda.

Then we eat. But not the ordinary way. He serves up my plate, and I serve up his. And we very carefully and sweetly feed each other each bite.

After breakfast, we lie back on the blanket, watch the clouds move into one animal shape and then another. And we hold hands, both wondering what the first kiss will feel like.

Diana, 17

"While many things are too strange to be believed, nothing is too strange to have happened."

Thomas Hardy

Write About the Extraordinary

Do you ever read the tabloids? Maybe skim the headlines while you're waiting in line at the grocery store? "Woman Gives Birth to Sixty-Pound Baby," "Man Captured by Aliens, Forced to Sing Patriotic Songs to Return to Earth," "Former Professional Wrestler Elected Governor" (actually, this one's true). Do you ever wonder where such bizarre stories come from?

Remarkable events occur around the world all the time. To find the unique and unusual, observe what's going on around you. What strange things have happened in your life? What

exceptional people do you know? What could your extraordinary story be about?

Granted, your extraordinary stories may not be about anything as bizarre as alien contact, but life has a way of present-
ing all kinds of strange-but-true incidents: a neighbor who
snores so loud you can hear him from inside your house or a
cousin who plays a song on the piano perfectly after hearing it
only once on the radio (and he's never had any music lessons).
Look into your past: maybe you have an ancestor who was a
famous actor or politician . . . or bank robber.

Explore the unusual or unexpected in your life and in your
writing. Stretch the truth a little, if you want to. Write a story so
far-fetched it would feel right at home in a tabloid.

"I take real people
and put them
in extraordinary
situations."

Robert Cormier

 WRITER'S CORNER

Turning Life into Fiction by Robin Hemley (Cincinnati, OH: Story Press, 1997).
This book shows how journal entries and real people, places, experiences, and
events from your own life can be turned into fiction.

 Write Now...

Write a "tabloid" story about yourself or a relative. What odd or
amazing traits run in your family? What incredible events have
taken place? If nothing immediately comes to mind, dig through
the past or talk to family members for some inspiration. Looking
through photo albums, old diaries, or baby books are great ways
to uncover information about your family's history.

Feel free to elaborate (even exaggerate) in your story. How
incredible can you make you or your relative appear? If you discover famous or notorious people in your family tree, you could
write about what it would be like to meet them today. What stories might they tell you about your other ancestors? How would
meeting these relatives influence your life? Do you feel proud
or maybe not-so-proud to have them as part of your history? Do
you see any similar qualities in yourself? What can you learn
from their lives?

Invent a Different You

As a creative writer, you have *poetic license,* or free rein, to create whatever scenario or situation you want in your writing. Unlike a journalist, who has to report the facts accurately, you have the freedom to add whatever details you want to get your point across. Because you aren't restricted to writing about how something *really* happened, how you acted, or what you felt, you can alter the outcome, change the characters involved, invent new places, and create new lives. You can start with something that's real and make it *un*real.

If you've always dreamed of being an astronaut, write about yourself as an astronaut. If you've ever considered joining a band, write about you and your bandmates on tour. If you've always wanted to be more outgoing or social, write about yourself as the life of the party. You can make anything "true" in your writing.

> "I think that the best thing about being a writer is that we get to make up things and tell the truth at the same time."
>
> Kyoko Mori

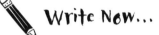 **Write Now...**

Imagine a life you could have lived if you weren't already living this one. Maybe you were born three hundred years ago in India to royalty, and your closest companion was a well-trained tiger. Or perhaps you were raised in Nova Scotia by a family who owns a whale-watching business. The possibilities are endless! Bring a new you to life on the page.

To narrow down your choices from the hundreds of ways your life could have turned out, try the following exercise: Get the Yellow Pages, a world atlas, and a dictionary. Turn to a random page of the phone book and, without looking, place your finger on an ad. In your written piece, this is where you'll be employed. You might be a hauler of large rocks, a plumber, a dermatologist, or a nightclub owner. Repeat this step using the world atlas. This is where you'll live. Maybe the Sandwich Islands, Tanzania, Antarctica, or Outer Mongolia will be your home. Next, randomly pick a word from the dictionary. This word will be relevant to your life somehow. Maybe the word is *bike* or *igloo*

Now construct a story fitting all the pieces of your "life" together. You might write about being a dermatologist somewhere in the Sandwich Islands, but your passion for bikes is getting in the way of your success because you're always leaving work early to go mountain biking.

Another variation of this exercise is to pick an article from a magazine like *National Geographic* and read about a place you've never visited. Write about what your life would be like if you lived there. What would you live in? What would you eat and how would you prepare your food? Who would your neighbors be? How would your family make a living? What would you learn about in school, or would you even go to school? Or pick a magazine that features celebrity teens. What would your life be like if you were famous?

It's hard being a cowgirl in Antarctica. For one thing, there are no horses here, and the polar bears just aren't the kind of animals you can saddle and ride around on yelling, "Yippee-i-yay." For another thing, I'm just kind of cold, working all day in the lab underground with the guys, and then sitting around at night in the center room, drinking endless hot chocolates while thinking of how much I miss my horse.

You see, horses are my great passion. They always have been, but I especially love palominos, like Linny back home in Montana. I think of how she would lift her head up whenever she saw me coming, and I wish we could be together again.

But I have to make do here—two more months, and then I'll have earned enough money to pay for all the rodeo fees for the next three years and for all the feed Linny can eat.

"There are many reasons why novelists write, but they all have one thing in common: a need to create an alternative world."

John Fowles

Meanwhile, I stare at the snow a lot. I feel
very alone and cold. I feel like I went to the end
of the world and fell off. And when I have time, I
knit socks for myself and all the guys—socks with
little horses on them.

Genevieve, 17

Add a Dash of Star Power

If you were told you could spend one day with any celebrity or fictional character—past or present—who would it be? Someone you consider your personal hero? A movie star? A politician? Your favorite author or character?

In your writing, you (or your characters) have the freedom to cross paths with anyone. You can make yourself Martin Luther King Jr.'s best friend, or Judy Blume's neighbor, or Steven Spielberg's kids' baby-sitter. A "My Worst Date" drama can become "My Worst Date with Rumpelstiltskin," or you could write about growing up with Bill Clinton as your father or Queen Elizabeth as your mother. Anything goes!

In the novel *Forrest Gump* by Winston Groom, the character Forrest chances upon many famous people during his life: a young and not-yet-famous Elvis Presley, John F. Kennedy, Richard Nixon, and John Lennon, just to name a few. Groom rewrites history pretending Forrest really existed and encountered these people. And author W. P. Kinsella, in his novel *Shoeless Joe,* writes about an ordinary farmer who receives a vision telling him to build a baseball diamond in the middle of his cornfield. Even though everyone thinks he's crazy, he builds the diamond and gets to meet one of his heroes, the legendary baseball player Shoeless Joe Jackson. (The movie *Field of Dreams* is based on this novel.) Like these writers, you can "change history."

So write about *your* day with your chosen celebrity. How do you happen to meet this person? What do you say to each

> "It's not enough to have imagination. You have to be able to tap into it."
>
> Stephen King

other? How do you spend the day together? Is he or she as nice, glamorous, smart, or funny as you expected? What do you learn from the experience?

Design Your Dream Home

If you could live anywhere, in anything, where would it be? Maybe a log cabin in the mountains, a treehouse, an open hut on an island, or a farmhouse in the country? Or maybe you'd rather live in a huge mansion, castle, or palace? Perhaps underground or on another planet?

At one time or another, almost everyone has imagined the perfect home. And why not? One day you may actually get to live in your dream home, so all this planning could come in handy.

Besides, you might get to know yourself a little better in the planning process. For example, if the home you design is a small cabin halfway up a mountain, this might reveal a love of nature and a need for solitude. On the other hand, if you imagine a large loft on the top floor of a New York City penthouse, this might show a desire to be close to the action and excitement of a big city. In your writing, you can investigate every nook and cranny, open every drawer and closet, and discover what makes this location a special place for you.

Write a description of your dream home. Is it big with an indoor pool, an exercise room, an indoor basketball court, a music studio, a library, and a private movie theater? Or is it smaller with just a bedroom, kitchen, bathroom, and writing room? Does it have a fireplace or hot tub? Does it have a porch or a deck or a patio? Do you keep a big grill or a hammock there? Do any pets or roommates live with you?

Did You Know?

The following are some of the authors who have had one or more of their books banned or burned at one time throughout the world: James Baldwin, Judy Blume, William Faulkner, Ernest Hemingway, Thomas Jefferson, J. D. Salinger, Harriet Beecher Stowe, Mark Twain, Walt Whitman, and Tennessee Williams.

Write About Wrongs

Do you feel strongly about a particular social issue? Is there a problem you want to take action against or help find a solution for? Maybe you're concerned about global warming, the situation in the Middle East, the destruction of the rain forests, or gun control. There are as many injustices in the world as there are raindrops, and they fall on people, animals, and the land all the time.

I remember watching my eight-year-old son write a long description about how solar cars could still run at night or when the sun is hidden behind the clouds. Through writing, he was able to come up with several creative ideas, some that might even work. Many writers use the written word to help them express their ideas, voice their opinions, and shed light on issues they believe in.

Writing about wrongs in your community, in your country, and on your planet is empowering. It allows you to explore the different sides of an issue and helps you figure out where you stand. When you imagine a potential solution to a problem, you're taking action. What could your next step be?

 **Write Now...**

Flip through any newspaper or news magazine and choose a story that interests you. It might be an article about people starving in developing countries, the percentage of students who passed mandatory academic tests, or this year's crime rate compared to last year's. Now focus on the problem the story reports. (As an alternative, simply select an issue or conflict you feel strongly about.)

Write about this problem, issue, or conflict as if it were already resolved. Describe how much better the world is without the problem (people in every nation have plenty to eat, all the students are passing their mandatory tests, and the crime rate is at an unprecedented low). Then trace the problem backwards and explain how it was fixed. What happened? Who took the initiative? How much time or money was spent on the solution? Where did the answers come from? What is known now that wasn't known before?

You just might find a solution that could work!

> "I don't think there is a political solution to the problems of man; I don't think there is a social solution. I think any solution is artistic."
>
> Gary Paulsen

Written as if the greenhouse effect were no longer an issue:

Life continues. The four seasons go on in the same
cycles they've run for thousands of years. We wear
some sunscreen in the summer, but we don't need to
be afraid of the sun all the time. The polar ice
caps stay frozen. And all because the greenhouse
effect is no longer a concern.

Yes, this would be life pretty much as we know
it except for one thing. We wouldn't drive cars
anymore. We would get to most places by bus
systems that were fixed up and improved in all the
cities and small towns. We would also travel by
trains once our rail system was updated and
enlarged to cover more of the country. In rural
areas like where I live, we would use horses, even
horse and buggies more. And we could still use
planes for long trips.

There might be some fossil-fuel-run vehicles,
like ambulances, school buses, and some cars used
only for emergency situations (located in the
center of each town where people could check them
out for short periods to go where no bus or train
or horse goes). But mostly we would travel by mass
transit. The good part is that people would get to
know each other more while riding buses and trains
to work and school each day. They might argue over
what radio station to play or what fast-food place
to drive through, but mostly, things would be a
lot better all around.

John, 16

Let the Two Sides Speak

Have you ever heard the expression "I'm of two minds about that"? If you're of two minds about something, it means you can't decide which side of an issue you support. Often, a right or wrong answer doesn't exist. You have to weigh the options and decide which solution offers the best outcome for everyone involved.

For example, consider the issue of animal rights. We use animals for medical research, which many people believe is cruel and inhumane. On the one hand, medical research on lab animals has led to the discovery of hundreds of cures that have saved thousands of human lives. On the other hand, what right do humans have to decide the fate of an animal, even if it's for a good cause? There's no clear right and wrong here, which makes the issue volatile.

When you're faced with an issue or decision, writing can help you figure out how to take action. This way, you can think through things, closely examine both sides of an issue, and debate the pros and cons on paper. Write about the different choices or options you have, or explore opposing sides of the issue. Are you of two minds? Or is there a clear "right" choice? Why or why not?

> "You're right from your side. I'm right from mine."
>
> Bob Dylan

Change the Rules

Rules—whether you like them or not—are a fact of life. Just about everywhere you go, you have to contend with rules. At school, you can't run in the hallways, you're expected to raise your hand to speak, and you need a hall pass to leave the class-room. Your parents probably provide you with a lot of rules, too: be home by a certain hour, finish your homework before watching TV, don't mouth off, be polite to your elders, and so on.

Society, in general, acknowledges certain rules and requires a code of behavior. It's customary, for example, to use a napkin when you eat, to face front when riding in an elevator, and to cover your mouth when coughing. You won't get in trouble with the law if you break any of these rules, but you could annoy or offend people.

> "There are no exceptions to the rule that everybody likes to be an exception to the rule."
>
> Charles Osgood

In addition to these rules, young people often add their own unspoken ones to the list. For instance, in order to hang out with a particular crowd at school, you might think you have to wear a certain brand of clothing or participate in specific activities.

In S. E. Hinton's book *The Outsiders,* the character Ponyboy writes about the unwritten rules that existed in his neighborhood when he was growing up. Kids were either a "Soc" or a "greaser," and whatever label you were given influenced your actions and other people's reactions: "Greasers are almost like hoods; we steal things and drive old souped-up cars and hold up gas stations and have a gang fight once in a while. . . . I'm not saying that either Socs or greasers are better; that's just the way things are."

Whatever the rules in your life are, writing about them can help you see how they affect your view of the world and yourself. You can think about the difference between rules that are trivial (don't chew gum in the classroom) and rules that save lives (don't drink and drive). Do rules help or hurt? How might you change any rules you disagree with?

"A writer's material is what he cares about."

John Gardner

Write Now...

Make a list of all the rules you're expected to follow in your life—rules made by parents, friends, teachers, coaches, lawmakers, and society. Are some rules easier to follow than others? Do you have to obey rules that seem to contradict each other? (For instance, maybe your mom believes you should always speak the truth, no matter what, but also makes you tell your uncle how much you like the present he gave you, even if you don't.)

Review your list and choose one rule to focus on. If you agree with the rule, talk about why it works for you. If you disagree with it (or keep breaking it), explain why. In what ways would you modify the rule, if you could?

How might you feel about this rule five, ten, or twenty years from now? Do you think you'd still hold the same opinion? What would make you change your mind? Write about it.

Written from the perspective of her twenty-five-year-old self, reflecting back to when she was a teen:

The big rule back then was that if you liked someone, you never told him directly. Instead, you got your best friend to talk to his best friend to "check out the scene" first. Then, if he said he liked you too, you acted nice to him, and when he said something about wanting your phone number, you said, "sure," as if it meant nothing to you.

In fact, you were supposed to act like you didn't care that much about going out with him all along, until it got really serious.

My problem was I couldn't deal with this rule. When I liked someone, I just went up to him and said, "I like you." If he said, "Cool," we went out. If he was freaked out, we didn't. But I didn't care because I was being true to myself, and I wasn't wasting my time waiting around for our best friends to sort it all out like they were our lawyers.

Actually, breaking this rule was good—it's how I met Brian. He wanted someone who would be honest, and so did I, so we started hanging out in tenth grade. Now, ten years later, we're married, and we have a five-year-old and another baby on the way.

We didn't have to play mind games for years before finding the "right one" because we were both ready to break the rules by being honest.

Gena, 14

Write on the Road

New places and faces can lead to new ideas, so try a change of environment. This doesn't mean you have to head off to some exotic locale (although it's great if you can!). Relaxing on a blanket in the park, riding a bus through the city, or sitting in a neighborhood coffee shop can expose you to new people, objects, and situations. Whether you're exploring the world or just the travel section of your local bookstore, keep your eyes open. Carry your journal or some paper with you at all times, so you can write about anything that inspires you.

A casual trip to the store or some other everyday place might not seem like it could inspire a life-changing event, but for a writer, anything is possible. Newbery Medal-winning author Cynthia Voigt, while walking into a grocery store, saw some kids who had been left in a car: she turned this observation into her first published novel, *Homecoming.* Children's book author J. K. Rowling was riding on a train between Manchester and London, England, when the idea for a series of books (beginning with *Harry Potter and the Sorcerer's Stone*) popped into her head. You never know when a great idea will strike.

Write Now...

Writing and travel are perfect companions, so take your writing on the road. Here are some places you might want to explore:

1. The zoo. Find an animal you enjoy watching and a comfortable place to sit (preferably out of the way of other visitors). Now describe:

- the animal and its actions, as if you're writing to someone who has never seen this animal before.

- a character you're inventing (even if the inventing starts at this moment) who has qualities very similar to the animal. For example, your character might walk like a gorilla or stand hunched over like a vulture.

2. A museum. Explore a museum of natural history, art, science, or local culture. Look for and write about:

- bones or artifacts on exhibit. Find a display you think is interesting, and write about what life was like for the people or creatures in that particular time and place.

"I've no idea where ideas come from and I hope I never find out; it would spoil the excitement for me if it turned out I just have a funny little wrinkle on the surface of my brain which makes me think about invisible train platforms."

J. K. Rowling

- a painting, sculpture, or photograph that you like. Imagine being the creator of this artwork—what were you thinking the moment you made it?

- any object that intrigues you—an old train, a tepee, a quilt. Think about who originally made or used the object. What was it like long ago?

3. The great outdoors. Head to a local park or nature trail, and find a place to sit and watch the activities going on around you. (Bring water, bug spray, sunscreen, something comfortable to sit on, and anything else you may need.) Relax, take in the scene around you, and write about:

- this spot as it may have looked one hundred, five hundred, or even one thousand years ago.

- one of the plants, animals, rocks, or other nearby elements. For fun, write from the perspective of a tree, or imagine you're in a snakeskin and see what happens!

- the people you see. What are they doing, thinking, and feeling at this moment?

Written as if the writer were a snake:

```
I wake and stretch out of my obsidian
circle. I open my mouth to many times its size
closed when only my tongue
darts and curls quick silver its yellow fork.
One part of me rushes forward. The other part
     catches up.
All day through the noise of the grass.
The heat warming my diamondback skin
until I disappear
underground.
                                        Brad, 15
```

CHAPTER 5

The Material of Your Life

When you look at your own life as a source of inspiration for your writing, you discover the experiences, ideas, thoughts, feelings, challenges, and hopes that contribute to who you are. Within the details of your day-to-day life lie the riches for your *writing* life. So dive deep into yourself, exploring things you've lived through, felt, thought, and known, and in the process, you may learn more about what you value, what you need, and what you can give to the world.

Words can be agents of change. When you write about what you want and what you dream of, these desires start to seem more real (because if you can put them into words, you can also begin to see ways to make them come true). You can use writing to help you focus on your dreams, sort through your feelings, figure out who you are, and make sense of your life. This is the power of language.

> "Life is all memory except for the one present moment that goes by so quickly you can hardly catch it going."
>
> Tennessee Williams

Special Correspondent at Your Own Birth

What if at your time of birth you had full language skills and a miniature microphone in your tiny hand? You could have recorded, moment by moment, the amazing details of the day you were born.

Telling the tale of your birth can help you better understand your roots. It's the story—the celebration—of you making your way out into the wider world. Writing about this event helps you learn more about how your life started and how you got where you are right now. While exploring your origins, you may begin to see the forces that, over time, have shaped and molded you.

 Write Now...

Start by doing research. Talk to your mom, dad, or another person who was present the day you were born. Or look at any records that offer you a glimpse of that day: your birth certificate, adoption records (if you have access to them), a baby book. Write down any significant details.

Now use your imagination to picture the room where you were born. Was it a hospital room, a room in someone's home, perhaps even an elevator or a taxi? Was the setting lit by fluorescent lights or sunshine? Describe the scene in vivid detail. Who was there waiting for your arrival? Describe the birth process as you might have felt it: Did it hurt? Was it fast, slow, or somewhere in between? Did you resist? Did you help push yourself out?

Imagine yourself at the very moment you left your warm cocoon for a new life outside. What did the rush of air feel like? Did your first exposure to light delight or annoy you? How did it feel to see your mom and to feel her touch for the first time, having known her up until this point only by the sound of her voice and the workings of her heart, lungs, stomach, and other organs?

Was your dad there to welcome you? Was some other special person there to wrap a blanket around you? Who held you first? What did you see when you opened your eyes? Capture it all on the page.

> "The first thing which I can record concerning myself is, that I was born. These are wonderful words. This life, to which neither time nor eternity can bring diminution—this everlasting living soul, began. My mind loses itself in these depths."
>
> Margaret Oliphant

```
I was born in the middle of summer in a very hot
room on the third floor of a hospital. And it all
happened very suddenly.
    One minute, I was with Mom at Dad's softball
game, sleeping and swimming quietly, feeling the
heat from the sun warm her and warm me. The next
thing I knew, Mom stood up to yell "Go for it!"
```

to Dad (he had just hit a triple, they told me
later), and she jumped up and down so much that my
little swimming pool started to leak.

Dad stopped running the bases, Mom started
crying a little, and someone drove us to the
hospital. I tried to tell Mom it would be fine,
they would just fill up the swimming pool again,
and we could go on like we had been for months and
months. But she wouldn't listen.

Soon we were in a quiet room, and Dad was
talking to Mom about how everything would be okay.
I kept waiting for someone to come with a hose to
put the water back in, but no one did. And even
worse, after a while, the walls started moving.

"Get some new water in here! The pool is
collapsing!" I wanted to yell, but since I couldn't
talk yet, I wasn't getting anywhere.

But anywhere was getting me. The walls got
tighter and tighter, and I heard Mom make strange
sounds, kind of like a cross between a moo and a
yell. I would get squeezed so tight I thought my
bones would break, and then everything would stop
for a moment. Then the squeezing would start again.

Pretty soon, the squeezing started pushing me
down a narrow passage. Down and tighter, tighter
and down . . . until I saw something very bright,
so bright it hurt my eyes.

It was the world.

Someone pulled me out by my shoulders and put
me facedown on Mom's stomach. She looked at me,
and I looked at her, and even though we had never
actually seen each other before, we knew who the
other was right away.

I heard Dad's voice, and then his big face looked
at me, too. Then someone wrapped me in a soft white
blanket and put me in Mom's arms. Mom and Dad held
me and cried and said my name over and over.

Diana, 17

"Just as our
historical begin-
nings are utterly
mysterious—why
are we born? why
when and as we
are?—so too are
the beginnings of
works of art and
of 'artists.'"
Joyce Carol Oates

Your Own Lullaby

At some point, each of us needs to be soothed, comforted, and told that everything will be all right. Sometimes the stresses of growing up make you feel like you're going out of your mind, and you need to find a little corner of the world that's loving, gentle, and accepting. Your writing can be this corner. You can write about what's bothering you, driving you crazy, or making you angry, sad, or confused. And then you can write yourself a lullaby.

Lullabies are songs that soothe. They inspire babies to calm down, stop crying, relax, and go to sleep. Lullabies help babies feel cuddled, loved, and embraced by someone who cares.

What does this have to do with you? You can write a lullaby to yourself in the form of a song, poem, story, or letter. Or you could even create a dialogue between your frenzied, worried self and your quiet, calm self. This lullaby can help you identify what brings you peace and makes you feel safe and secure. Store your lullaby in a private place and read it whenever you feel upset, unsure, or in need of comfort.

Sometimes just the act of writing the lullaby is soothing and calming. If you're worked up about something, see if writing helps calm you down. If this doesn't work for you, try exercising, talking to a friend, or breathing deeply. (See the deep-breathing exercise on page 93.)

 **Write Now...**

Lullabies are designed to be lulling. Even the word *lullaby* is soft and soothing. The words in any given lullaby are usually soft, too, melting into one another, and emphasizing vowel sounds. You rarely hear sharp words like *racket* or *thunderclap* in a lullaby. Instead you hear gentle ones like *hush, sleep, baby, slumber, wish, moon,* and *dream.* As you write your lullaby, use gentle, quiet words.

```
Go to sleep, you tired one.
Close your eyes and rest your soul.
Sleep and know your life is good.
Sleep until the new day comes.
                              Cara, 16
```

For fun, you can let loose and take this exercise one step further. Circle every verb (action word) in your lullaby; then look at the letter of the alphabet each one starts with. (Example: *rest* begins with *R*.) For each circled verb, substitute a verb that begins with the *next* letter of the alphabet. So, if your word started with *R,* search for a word starting with *S.* (Tip: Choose verbs that sound soothing and calming, but don't spend time trying to figure out if they make sense in your lullaby.) Write each new word above the circled word it's replacing.

Listen to what happens when you read your revised lullaby. Do the word changes surprise you? Do they add new meaning? A new twist? Do they tell you something about yourself?

```
Hide in sleep, you tired one.
Darken your eyes and soothe your soul.
Turn and learn your life is good.
Turn until the new day dawns.
                              Cara, 16
```

84

Write from Your Dreams

In Xanadu did Kubla Khan
A stately pleasure-dome decree:
Where Alph, the sacred river, ran
Through caverns measureless to man
   Down to a sunless sea.

> "I had a dream with something salvageable in it, and I said: 'Oh, that's wonderful, what a great idea.'"
>
> Stephen King

So begins the poem "Kubla Khan, or a Vision in a Dream, a Fragment," written by English poet Samuel Taylor Coleridge during the Romantic Era (late 1700s, early 1800s). It was inspired by a dream he had. In his dream, he had a vision of Xanadu, a splendorous place inhabited by one of the great Khans of Mongolia when Mongolia ruled a large portion of the world. When he awoke, Coleridge grabbed some paper and started scribbling down words to capture his vision.

But before he finished the poem, he was interrupted by a visitor. When he returned to complete the poem, he no longer remembered the rest of his vision: the poem was left unfinished, a fragment.

Courtesy of the unconscious, dreams let you experience reality on another channel, and even if you can't control the "programming," you *can* take what you experience in dreams and apply it to your writing. Dreams can reveal words, images, or sounds that give you clues about what to write, how to phrase a sentence, or what to title something. Dreaming restocks your deep well of creativity while you sleep, potentially supplying new images, characters, or scenes you can use in your writing. The possibilities are as varied as your dreams.

Suppose you have a dream about taking an important exam: You sit at a desk, look at your test, and realize it's written in Spanish. But you're not in Spanish class and you don't speak the language at all! Sound familiar? Use a dream like this as the inspiration for a story, perhaps about someone attempting to take a test but encountering every delay and conflict imaginable. Or write an essay about test anxiety—the quicksand-sinking feeling you get in the pit of your stomach and how this can make it so much harder to get through the test.

Many writers keep a journal or notebook next to their bed so, as soon as they wake up, they can record ideas that come to them in the night. Like Coleridge's vision, dreams can be fleeting: capture them on the page so they don't slip away.

 ## WRITER'S CORNER

The Dreamer's Companion: A Young Person's Guide to Understanding Dreams and Using Them Creatively by Stephen Phillip Policoff (Chicago: Chicago Review Press, 1997). A guide to the mysterious world of the subconscious, this book explores how dreams have shaped history and how to interpret your own dreams.

The Dream Scene by Alison Bell (Los Angeles: Lowell House Juvenile, 1994). This book can help you learn how to interpret your dreams, keep a dream journal, and use dreams to help solve problems.

 ## Write Now...

Writing from your dreams not only inspires ideas but also brings new insight into how you think and feel, and what you desire or fear. Sometimes, dreams evoke images and emotions so intense that when you wake, it's difficult to know whether what happened *really* happened or not.

To write from your dreams:

• Take an image, a character, an incident, an object, a setting, or a feeling from a dream you've had and explain it in your writing. What do you think the meaning of the dream might be? Does a person or object in the dream represent something other than who or what it is?

• Some people believe that the characters in dreams represent different aspects of your personality. To explore this theory, write

> "The dream ...
> is a message
> of yourself
> to yourself."
>
> Fritz Perls

a dialogue among the characters in a dream of yours, assuming they're different parts of yourself. Try to figure out what part of your personality each character represents.

To blend reality and dreams together:

- Take a real incident or event and write about it as if it were a dream. For example, maybe you saw the movie *Titanic* with a blind date who had very bad breath, kept leaning on your arm rest, and wouldn't share any popcorn. Because you're transforming your real life into the dreamworld, you could blink your eyes and exchange this less-than-dreamy date for Leonardo DiCaprio or Kate Winslet. It's your dream, so anything can happen!

Visit Your Inner Older Man or Woman

"When I am an old woman I shall wear purple" begins the poem "Warning" by Jenny Joseph. Do you ever wonder what *you'll* be like when you get older? Will you wear funky clothes? Will you enjoy the same kind of foods and music that you enjoy now? Will you act like your parents or grandparents? How will you spend your time?

While you might hear some adults say they're getting in touch with their *inner child,* I find it more valuable to hang out with my inner *older* self instead. I imagine visiting my older woman in a quaint little cottage in the woods where "she" enjoys cooking potato-and-cheese casseroles and reading all day. During our conversations, she likes to get right to the point and can be a little abrupt sometimes—but then so can I, which is probably why we understand each other so well.

Visiting your older self is like time-traveling into the future. You get to meet the person you'll become years down the road and even find out what you have to look forward to in the future: where you'll work, who or if you'll marry, successes you'll experience, and obstacles you'll have to overcome. Having a dialogue with someone who's so similar to yourself, but older and wiser, can help you discover the type of person

> "As I approve of a youth that has something of the old man in him, so I am no less pleased with an old man that has something of the youth. He that follows this rule may be old in body, but can never be so in mind."
>
> Marcus T. Cicero

you want to be, what matters most to you in life (happiness? career? family? fame?), and how to define your future goals.

Write Now...

Imagine visiting your inner older self at different ages in your life: ten years from now, then twenty, thirty, and so on. What do you look like at each age? Where do you live? What kind of home do you have? Do you live alone? Do you work, or are you retired? What is or was your profession?

Imagine the conversation between the two of you. What do you need each other to know? What insights and advice can your older self give you? What personality traits do you currently have that you still want to have when you're older?

Feel free to revisit your inner older self anytime to see how much you both have learned since you last got together.

> "We grow neither better nor worse as we get old, but more like ourselves."
>
> May L. Becker

The forest opens to a sea of black, and on the north beach there is a house glowing with light from its many windows. I admire the beautiful and exotic colors that come from the stained-glass windows from the top of the house. Inside is a smell so delicious its fragrance could feed a thousand people. I knock on the old brass door, and it opens. An old woman standing behind it invites me into her warm home that smells of apples, cinnamon, and honey. The kind woman tells me of her years and accepts my gift of colored stones and pebbles. Her endless tales are filled with beauty and magic. And her stories of the black sea bring back familiar memories of my past.

Erin, 12

Write Your Life Backwards

Did you ever see the *Seinfeld* episode called "The Betrayal," where Jerry, George, and Elaine are in India for their friend's wedding? The whole episode is told backwards. It starts with the closing credits and ends with the opening theme music.

The first scene of this episode shows the gang sitting in the coffee shop talking about the wedding they attended, and the final scene takes place eleven years *earlier* when Jerry first meets his neighbor Kramer. The ending is actually the beginning. The sitcom writers worked their way back so the beginning became the end. Sound confusing? It's not, really. Every scene starts earlier in time than the scene before it and explains what events led up to the previous scene. The episode was inspired by Harold Pinter's play *The Betrayal,* which also is told backwards.

Most stories go forward in time: you pick a place to start and tell what happens next, and next, until you reach the ending. Sometimes a story might start with the ending, flash back to the beginning, and work its way forward to the ending. Or a story might start in the middle, jump back to the beginning, move forward to the middle again, and continue on to a new and exciting ending.

But it's rare to find a story that tells itself backwards. Telling a story this way can help you see the cause behind the effect. When you unravel why this or that happens, you discover, kind of like a detective, a mystery's point of origin. Writing backwards helps you see how your mind puts a story together and where the story came from in the first place.

> "To look backward for a while is to refresh the eye, to restore it, and to render it the more fit for its prime function of looking forward."
>
> Margaret Fairless Barber

> "We need the rock of the past under our feet in order to spring forward into the future."
>
> Madeleine L'Engle

Write Now...

Think of something that's happened in your life recently and write about it backwards. Maybe you won first place at a science fair, or you sprained your ankle, or you finished another school year.

How do you write about it backwards? Well, it's not like *sdrawkcab.* Instead, start with the final result and then add what came before it, and before that, and even before that. Make sure you provide the connective threads that weave the story together. As you write, ask yourself why certain events led to others. What choices or decisions influenced what happened? Knowing what you know now, would you make the same choices again? Why or why not?

Family Writes

I once knew a young woman who was adopted by alcoholic parents who died before she was fourteen. She spent her teen years going from orphanage to orphanage until she was old enough to live on her own. Writing about these experiences—the regrets, anger, sadness, funny moments, and daydreams of what it would have been like to grow up in a different family—not only made for a great story but also helped release her from the pains of her past.

Many writers regard the ups and downs of family life as prime material for their writing. Glance through the autobiog-raphy section of your local library and you'll discover *hundreds* of authors who write about their own lives, from the time they were children to the days when they had their own children, or even grandchildren. You can read all about what other

people—famous ones—have gone through in their own family lives. You'll see that families come in all shapes and sizes, and have their own sets of problems and ways of dealing with them.

Our families can be the best and worst thing that ever happened to us. Maybe your parents drive you crazy with all their rules; maybe your siblings borrow your stuff without asking or seem to always be in competition with you. On the other hand, maybe they're the people who give you unconditional love and support, and who are there for you in your worst time of need. What do you love about your family? What don't you love about them? How do they act, and why? What do you do together?

> "It's very hard as an autobiographer to be present in the past; almost impossible. And yet it is only when the autobiographer can achieve that impossibility that one approaches the success of literature."
>
> Maya Angelou

90

What don't you do together? What would you change about them? What would you leave the same?

Think about a major event (positive or negative) that occurred in your family. What crazy, exciting, scary, maddening, or inspiring family episode could you share? What makes this recollection meaningful to you? Did it change your life or family in some way? If so, how?

For fun, imagine you're writing your autobiography. What would you want people to know about your family? What *wouldn't* you want them to know?

WRITER'S CORNER

How to Write Your Own Life Story: The Classic Guide for the Nonprofessional Writer by Lois Daniel (Chicago: Chicago Review Press, 1997). This book helps you start writing your own story, with topics that trigger memories and help you discover meaningful events in your life. It includes real samples from other people's autobiographies.

Inventing the Truth: The Art and Craft of Memoir edited by William Zinsser (Boston: Houghton Mifflin Company, 1998). In this book, nine well-known authors describe the pleasures and problems of writing a memoir, and how to impose a structure on experiences, memories, and emotions of the past.

Through My Eyes: A Journal for Teens by Linda Kranz (Flagstaff, AZ: Rising Moon, 1998). The thought-starters on lined pages in this book encourage you to write about your relationships with your family, friends, and yourself. The blank pages provide space to record your memories.

Writing for Your Life: A Guide and Companion to the Inner Worlds by Deena Metzger (San Francisco: Harper San Francisco, 1992). This book features hundreds of writing exercises that inspire creative thinking and help writers see all the sources of stories in their own lives.

Your Personal Landscape

Each person has his or her own specific, one-of-kind *landscape.* Think of this landscape as a map of who you are and where you've been. Your personal landscape is your territory, complete

> "I felt uncomfortable in setting out to write about Native American life, so I didn't for a long time. But it became impossible to deny. I mean, you can't deny your own background."
>
> Louise Erdrich

with unexplored regions, scenic spots, secret caves, and inter-esting paths, byways, side streets, and corners. Why not write a travel guide about this territory? Tell who you are as if you're describing a vast and intricate landscape, one that may have swamps, mountains, beaches, prairies, parking lots, or thick forests.

By describing the landscape of who you are, you come to discover all kinds of new terrain. You can learn more about where you've traveled in your life, where you're going, and where you are now.

 ## Write Now...

First, draw an imaginary landscape of your name. Use crayons, markers, colored pencils, pens, paint, whatever you want. Draw where the land rises and falls, what's built where, what animals populate the land, and where the rivers, highways, and dirt roads are.

Next, write the landscape of your name. That is, take your name (first, last, middle, or whatever you want to call yourself) and pretend it's the name of a newly discovered place on the earth. Describe to your reader what this place is like.

> "And because I found I had nothing else to write about, I presented myself as a subject."
>
> Montaigne

```
People who come to Judy have a hard time finding
their way home again. That's because Judy is such
a crowded and busy place in its center, and so
full of obstacles all around its center. There are
mud pits, snakes in the grass, barbed wire, and
wild dogs all over.
    I myself get lost in Judy all the time. I drop
in, looking for a good tree to take a nap under,
and before I know it, I'm woken up by herds of
buffalo shaking the ground. "Oh, there go my fears
again," I think.
                                    Judy, 16
```

Body "Talk"

Poet and fiction writer Sandra Cisneros has a chapter in *The House on Mango Street* called "Hips." Her main character, Esperanza, describes to her friends how hips suddenly appear "like a new Buick with the keys in the ignition." With the arrival of hips comes the need for some knowledge: "You gotta be able to know what to do with hips when you get them, I say making it up as I go. You gotta know how to walk with hips, practice you know—like if half of you wanted to go one way and the other half the other." By focusing on one body part this way, the author paints a vivid picture of the excitement and mystery of growing up and becoming a woman.

Listen to what your own stomach, toes, elbows, or neck are saying to you—you just might learn something about yourself. An injured knee, for example, may reveal that you push yourself too hard. Strong shoulders might show that you can be counted on for support or that you can handle a lot of responsibility. You can write about a body part or physical feature you really like, or perhaps one you don't like. What do these features say about you?

Imagine yourself in the body part you're writing about—feel what it's like to live life from that perspective. For example, you could write about the secret life of your feet, taking a look at what it's like to live so close to the ground all day long: "Back into those hard black shoes. Why us? Haven't we suffered enough in old socks for three days? And now he stands on us again, lifts us up and puts us down, over and over. Most days we get a little seasick and need to dangle for a while to recover."

Write Now...

Use the following steps to help you relax and free your mind. Read through all the directions first, and then try the exercise. If you prefer, ask someone to read the steps aloud to you, or tape-record them and play them back to yourself.

Did You Know?

Amy Tan's second novel, *The Kitchen God's Wife*, was inspired by the real-life events of her mom, Daisy. While living in China, Daisy divorced her abusive husband but lost custody of her three daughters. She had to leave her daughters behind when she fled from the Communist takeover in 1949. Daisy's second marriage was to John Tan, and they had three children together: Amy and her two brothers.

1. Get comfortable and close your eyes. Notice where your weight is settling into the furniture, or floor, and where you feel tense or relaxed.

2. Breathe slowly and deeply.

3. Imagine that each time you inhale, a golden light enters your body through the soles of your feet, travels up your legs to the base of your spine, and moves through your spine to the top of your head.

4. When you exhale, imagine the golden light fountaining out the top of your head and returning back toward the ground, enveloping your whole body as the light falls to the floor. (After a few minutes of breathing like this, you should feel calmer and more relaxed.)

5. Now focus on the part of your body that calls to you. Ask it to tell you its story, and let it have its say. Describe its history— what it's been through, what's caused it problems, and how it gets through an average day.

I'm tired of holding everything together—that big head of yours above and that busy body below. It's a big responsibility to only be five inches long and yet have to link all the heavier bones. Speaking of which, you may be pleased at those heavier shoulders, but I'm not. Put down those weights! They make me have to pull and pull with all my might, so that your head doesn't crash into your chest.

   And sit up straight, too! You think this slumping over is fun, but it twists me up in ways that hurt for days. One other thing while we're talking—two words: No turtlenecks. Those things make me feel like I'm being suffocated.

Brad, 15

As an alternative to this exercise, you can choose a part of your body and think about what type of animal resides there. This sounds strange, but it can be fun! Over the years, I've heard my students say they found a great blue heron in their heart, an evil monkey in their back, or a gentle llama in their neck. All these inner animals showed the students something surprising about themselves.

Start with the relaxation exercise on page 93, and then imagine what kind of animal might live in the body part you choose. Ask the animal for its story, its likes and dislikes, its successes and failures. What can this animal teach you about yourself?

Did You Know?

The Brontë sisters, Charlotte, Emily, and Anne, authors of *Jane Eyre, Wuthering Heights,* and *Agnes Grey* (respectively), wrote using the pseudonyms Currer, Ellis, and Acton Bell. In 1848, Charlotte and Anne revealed their true identities to their publisher in order to prove that they were, in fact, two separate authors, and not one author writing under two pseudonyms, as one American publisher suspected.

I used to see a very frantic gorilla in my head when I did this exercise. His name was Sid, and he felt so driven to make things, clean rooms, take baths, polish floors. "Sid, relax a little," I'd say. But this gorilla was wound a little too tight to hear a soothing comment.

So one day I visualized Sid climbing into a hot tub, while I told him he needed and deserved a little break. Afterwards, I led him to a sheepskin rug to lie upon, and I played him a great CD until he fell asleep.

Both Sid and I felt a lot calmer after that.

Cara, 16

Put on Your Favorite Mask

Have you ever had to act or pretend to be something or someone you're not? Maybe you pretended to enjoy bowling, so you wouldn't feel left out at the party your friends organized at the local alley. Or you bumped into the girl you have a crush on, but she was with a big group of friends, so you acted like you didn't have any special feelings for her. These are examples of wearing different *masks,* or changing a little bit about yourself, depending on the social situation you're in.

Everybody wears a mask at some point. Sometimes you feel too scared to show your true self. At other times, life requires you to act a certain way, even when you don't feel like it. For example, if you're having a rotten day and are feeling down, but you have a job interview, you need to wear a mask that shows your prospective employer you're competent, confident, positive, and upbeat. You can't let what's inside show on the outside. Your mask hides the truth.

When you explore the different masks you've worn at different times, you learn how outside forces influence the way you feel, the way you respond to others, and how much of your true self you're willing to share. Why did you put on the mask? What did it look like? How did you feel while wearing it? Do other people you know wear masks? Why? What does this tell you about them?

My mask is made of blue and purple feathers with tiny seashells glued around the edges. It looks beautiful, especially when I'm wearing it at night, and the feathers look iridescent.

When you see me in my mask, you might think I look this way all the time—feathery and light, yet with shining dark colors. You might think that I can fly very high and yet my love is the ocean. And all these things you might think are true.

But without my mask, I look very different. I have brown eyes that usually look down into books. I don't decorate my face with colors.

Without my mask, I don't make myself up for the world. Instead, I'm quiet. I'm usually reading a book. And inside my head, I'm writing my own book. Inside that story, people don't wear masks at all. They scream and cry and make fools of themselves. And still they shine.

Jon, 15

"Our masks, always in peril of smearing or cracking, in need of continuous checks in the mirror or silverware, keep us in thrall to ourselves, concerned with our surfaces."

Carolyn Kizer

Make Your Wish

Have you ever wished upon a star? Or dug through your pockets for a penny to throw into a wishing fountain? What did you wish for? A new car? A million dollars? An *A* on your English test? World peace? You don't have to wait for the birthday candles to be blown out or for a star to fall in order to make wishes.

In your writing, you can wish as often as you want. And you can write about what might happen if your wishes really came true. How would your life change? How would *you* change?

When you write about your wishes, you're able to express what's important to you and why. You start thinking about what you hope to achieve, and sometimes just putting these thoughts into words can motivate you to take action. Then you can figure out what steps you need to take to make your wishes come true for real.

Write Now...

Make a list of everything you wish for, practical or not-so-practical. Maybe you want to grow another six inches, be the best trombone player in the state, have a date for the movies Friday night, or get into a good college. Once you've expressed all your wishes, put your list away and don't look at it for a week or so.

```
I wish to feel accepted and loved by my family,
even my stepfather.

I wish to pass my driver's test and get my license
within a year.

I wish for the patience and perseverance to study
everything I care about with all my heart and
soul, even when it is difficult.

I wish to continue my close friendships and find new
friends who share my love of writing and painting.

I wish to write every week for at least two hours
and to appreciate whatever I can write in that time.

I wish for my grandmother to feel better.

I wish for a good part-time job doing something I
like, so that I can save money for a car (I also wish
for a good music store or coffee shop to hire me).

I wish for true love, but only when it's the right time.

I wish for feeling like I belong at my new school.

                                         Naomi, 14
```

"Live the questions now. Perhaps then, someday far into the future, you will gradually, without even noticing it, live your way into the answer."

Rainer Maria Rilke

When you return to your wish list, revise it while keeping the following ideas in mind:

- Make sure everything on your list really is something you want. Imagine what could happen if a wish came true. Would there be consequences you haven't considered?

- Rephrase any negative language in positive ways. In other words, if you wish for something *not* to happen, reword the wish so it focuses on what you *want* to happen. For instance, your wish might be to not fail your driver's test. Change that into your wish to pass it (or ace it!).

After revising your list, go one step further: turn your wishes into goals. To make a wish into a goal, you have to be ready to *take action* to accomplish something. You don't let fate decide whether your wishes will come true.

First, write down your goal, and make it specific and clear; this is your long-term goal. Next, list the steps you need to take to help you meet it; these are your short-term goals. For example, your long-term goal might be to become a great guitar player. Your short-term goals could be to (1) find a guitar that you can practice on, (2) get a good teacher, (3) learn a few chords, and (4) play a song. Writing down the steps you have to take along the way helps you stay on track and monitor your progress.

If you'd like, set some specific goals for your writing. What do you ultimately hope to achieve with it? Is it your dream to write a novel? Get published? Create a play and act in it, too? Sell the movie rights to your life story? Keep a set of journals that can be handed down to your great-great-grandchildren someday? Maybe write a Pulitzer Prize-winning poem? Whatever your writing goal may be, put it on paper. Think about the steps you need to take to reach your goal, and take the first one today.

PART 3

Surfacing:
The Vision of
Revision

*"Never think of revising as fixing something
that is wrong. That starts you off in a negative frame
of mind. Rather think of it as taking an opportunity
to improve something you already love."*

MARION DANE BAUER

Look at revision (re-*vision*) as your chance to see your work with
fresh eyes. In the process, you learn more about yourself, your
writing as it is now, and how you can take your writing further.
The writing process—writing something, shaping it, revising it,
and letting it venture out into the world—can sustain you far
more than just expressing yourself in one draft.

You review, reflect, reshape, rework, renew. Along the way, you learn more about what's important to you, how you work, and what your writing wants to say. You may labor for days, weeks, months (even years) over a piece of writing, but in the end, you bring your best work to the surface. And you taste the sweetness that persistence and courage, hard work and daring can bring.

CHAPTER 6

Learning to Revise

At this point, you've overcome a major obstacle: you found the courage to put something on paper. You dared to write. Now that you've come this far, there's less blocking your view, and your vision expands. *Revisioning* is a noun coined by poet Adrienne Rich, and it means looking at your writing and your life anew to see what's possible beyond the borders of time and convention.

In a way, revision is a relationship you forge with what you write, and as with any healthy relationship, there has to be some trust. Trust that what you've written has value, that it expresses your experiences, thoughts, and feelings. Trust, too, that you can take what you've written and express yourself more fully—with more purpose, precision, and power.

To revise, you must first look at your work as a whole—not pick it apart sentence by sentence and word by word. (That task comes later!) Ask yourself, "Does it say what I want it to say? How might I say it better?" A good way to "hear" what your writing conveys is by reading it aloud. Even better, tape-record yourself reading your work out loud and then play it back. Listen carefully to the words, the pacing, the rhythms.

As you read through (or listen to) your story, poem, essay, or play, keep one important fact in mind: *You are not your writing.* True, the characters may look like you or think what you think. They may even feel what you feel. The setting may closely resemble your home. Certain plot twists might be based on things that have happened in your own life. Still, you are not your writing.

> "No writing has any real value which is not the expression of genuine thought and feeling."
>
> Eleanor Roosevelt

Why is it important to remember this? Because if you believe that you are your writing, then it's painful to revise anything you write. Changing a line is like getting a paper cut. Cutting a passage is like giving blood. Killing a big hunk of a story is like breaking a leg. And you've got better things to do than to feel pain.

Believing that you are your writing may prevent you from doing what's best in the revision process. Revision is all about *daring*—daring to let your creativity run wild all over again, to cut away what doesn't feed the soul of the piece, and to listen to what the writing wants to say and be.

Also, if you believe you are your writing, then you'll probably take any critique of your work as a criticism of you. Suppose you hand your friend your finished story, and after she reads it she says, "I liked the opener, but then I got bored." Does this mean your friend thinks you're boring? Of course not! But unless you have some distance from what you write, it's hard to hear anything but your own painful reaction to other people's comments.

> "I can't write five words but that I change seven."
>
> Dorothy Parker

The converse is also true. "I love your writing" or "This is one of the best things I've ever read" might be a great compliment for *any* writer to hear. There's nothing wrong with feeling good about yourself if you receive this type of praise, unless this is the *only* way you prove to yourself that you're worthy. If you write for love and attention, you run the risk of seeing your art ONLY as a way to prove your worth, and this will keep your writing from growing into its best form.

For many years (although I would have denied it then if you had asked me), I wrote to be loved. I thought that if I made something beautiful on paper, I was worthy of people truly loving me. I showed my poetry to people I cared about, hoping they would read it and be so amazed that they would keep caring about me. You know what? It didn't work.

The people who loved me did so for *me*—not for my poetry. If I wrote garbage, they still loved me. (What a relief!) I came to realize that I'm far more than my writing.

You are, too. Writing is a two-dimensional thing on a page; it may feel alive in some ways, but it isn't a living being like you. You are alive *off* the page.

This brings us back to the beginning: You dared to write. Now you can dare to *rewrite*.

Build It Up and Knock It Down

"Build it up and knock it down" is wise advice from the late Jane Kenyon, an American poet. She meant that after you write everything you possibly can on the winds of impulse and drive (build it up), you then edit out all you possibly can (knock it down). You build and rebuild until the piece "feels" right.

Think of this process as a kind of "slashing and burning" that clears away deadwood and makes room for the lush green of new sprouts to push through the dirt.

But how do you light this fire in the first place? Here are thirteen tips to get started:

1. Copy your work by hand or on the computer. (This works best if the piece is short!) You may be surprised at what words you add in or take out, consciously or unconsciously.

2. Create a balance. Be sure the most important scenes, characters, descriptions, and images carry the most weight in your work. Is your main character overshadowed by a secondary character who seems to get all the good lines? Do your descriptions of minor events drag on, slowing the action of the story? Cut what you don't need.

3. Don't explain too much. Have you explained far too much to your reader? Have you *told* rather than *shown?* (For more about "Show, don't tell," see pages 47–48.) For example, if a certain character in your story is a villain, say so with a gesture: "He kicked his dog with the toe of his snakeskin boot." Avoid explaining to your readers that "Mr. Meany was very cruel." Trust your images *and* your reader's ability to understand them.

4. Go with the flow. Each scene of your story, each stanza of your poem, should flow seamlessly into the next. *Flow* is about bridging any gaps in your writing. If, for example, the plot

"Own anything you want in your writing and then let it go!"

Natalie Goldberg

doesn't follow a logical sequence, your readers might get lost. And if your dialogue doesn't read smoothly, your readers may not know who's speaking and why. Your words should provide a smooth path for readers to follow.

5. Listen to the beat. All writing has its own rhythm. If you read something aloud and tap out the beats (the accented syllables), you can hear the rhythm. Listen to the beat of your words. If you hear a false note, a missing beat, or a jumble of noise in a passage that was supposed to be quiet, then work on the rhythm. Cut or add words where you see fit. Choose words with more vowels or consonants to produce the "sound effect" you want.

6. Be precise. Your words and images should convey exactly what you want them to. This makes your writing vivid. In the knock-it-down process, you might change "the big tree" to "the enormous sycamore." You might describe a "beautiful sunset" as "rays of scarlet and gold." Precision counts.

7. Remember that once is enough. When you read over your work, watch for redundancy. Don't keep describing the tree as "the canopy of leaves"—a once-fresh image can go stale fast. Have you mentioned your character's lovely brown eyes ten times? In dialogue, have you needlessly repeated "said so-and-so" again and again? Cut it out!

8. Less is more. One clear, vivid image will affect your reader more powerfully than long passages of description. Overdone descriptions are like a tangle of weeds choking the grass. You may feel attached to some of your more "poetic" language, but ask yourself if it truly moves your story or poem along. (For more on this, see "File Away Your 'Darlings'" on pages 129–130.)

9. Avoid passive voice. Good writing is *active;* it relies on strong verbs (action words). Do a lot of your sentences use some form of the "to be" verb?

As in: *He was walking to the store to find out if his sister was going to be off of work soon.*

> "The difference between the right word and the nearly right word is the same as that between lightning and the lightning bug."
>
> Mark Twain

Or: *She was met at the store by her brother.*

Instead, how about: *He walked to the store to meet his sister, who usually got off work at noon.*

Hunt for lazy sentences that use too many *is, was,* and *were* verbs. In general, *gerunds* (verbs ending with "ing") indicate passive language, so change these verbs to a more active form (*talking* becomes *talk*).

10. Be direct. Some sentences seem to go on and on, as if they have a lot to say, when really they could have conveyed the original idea in a much more succinct and brief way than how they were presented (do you get the point?). Good writing is direct and clear.

11. Test-drive your dialogue. Read your dialogue aloud to see if it sounds real. Is the language accurate for the character? Do the words reflect your character's age, background, and personality?

12. Check your punctuation. Punctuation should work for you, not against you. For example, if you use too many commas, your readers may be distracted or slowed down. And if you use a semicolon where you need a colon, or have no comma where there should be one, you'll probably end up confusing your readers.

It's exciting to type exclamation points!! They can make your writing seem as if it's bubbling with joy or seething with anger, but if you use too many, you dilute their power. Save exclamation points for when they're most needed, and they'll have a greater impact.

If you're interested in experimenting with punctuation, first make sure you're familiar with common punctuation rules, so you know how and why you're breaking them (and so your reader has a chance of understanding what you're doing, too).

13. If you're writing poetry, think about line breaks. You can identify a poem, most of all, by how it sits on the page. Generally, poets break their lines (meaning they end one line

> "I was working on the proof of one of my poems all morning, and I took out a comma. In the afternoon, I put it back again."
>
> Oscar Wilde

and go on to the next) in two ways. The first is to mimic the rhythm of speech, breaking the line where a person would naturally pause. The second way is to break a line to show some other meaning. For example, you might write . . .

> There stands my dad. A tall and protective
> tree shields me from the wind.

While "tall and protective" have to do with the tree, this description—because of where the line breaks—also reflects back on the poet's father.

To get a feel for the revision process in general, take a look at the following writing samples.

From a first draft (the build-it-up version):

```
Rain everywhere, staining the horizon all direc-
tions, the mist filling the field with blue shade,
the five large crows waiting atop the cedar tree.
Everything silent. Even me, waiting behind the
open sky, my face wet and young. Even if it's not
morning. Even if it's not yet evening. Even if
it's something between summer and fall, something
between horses in sunlight, grasshoppers humming
over there in the heated-up light and red leaves
just fallen, still damp over here in the cooler
brightness of fall. This in-between place, this
blue-air place, this waiting-crow place, this is
where I live. This is where I walk quietly,
wondering why I always have to be in between
child and adult, sleep and waking, knowing and
not knowing, and all the other places that don't
know my name.

                                        Cara, 16
```

From a redraft (a knock-it-down version):

```
Rain stains the horizon, mist fills the field with
blue shade. Five large crows wait atop the cedar
tree. Everything is silent. Even me, waiting behind
the open sky, my face wet and young. Not morning,
not evening, sometime between horses in sunlight,
grasshoppers humming in the summer light and damp
red leaves cooling on the ground. This in-between
place made of blue and waiting crow. This place
where I wait between child and adult, sleep and
waking, knowing and not knowing.

                                        Cara, 16
```

Make a Map of Your Writing

Suppose you've completed a first draft and you're reviewing what you've written, word by word—so many words—and you no longer seem to know what you're trying to say. How do you get to the point where you can see what you need to do?

All good writing needs to find and fit into its own shape. And all good writers need to discover ways to observe the "lay of the land" of what they write, so they can see its shape, its landscape. One way to get this overview is by making a mini-blueprint of what you've written.

A blueprint is like a map of a building. Your blueprint will be the map that guides you through your own writing. For example, if I were mapping this small section of the book, I might say:

- Paragraph 1: Introduction to topic of seeing your way through your writing.

- Paragraph 2: Writing needs to find its own shape, with help from the writer.

- Paragraph 3: Making a mini-blueprint helps.

> "It is not unusual to find one whole wall of my writing room plastered with current chapter outlines and storyboards."
>
> Janet E. Grant

Mapping is like making an outline *after* you've written something. Now you can just scan your outline and see what you've said, what still needs to be said, what could be said a little less. By looking at the whole landscape of your writing, you get a better idea of what direction the writing wants to take.

Focus In

As you think about ways to revise, polish, and strengthen your writing, focus in on passages you haven't concentrated on before. Think of your pen as a video camera and aim it in for a close-up. Focus on one image, one character, one line, one scene.

Suppose you decide to adjust your lens to hone in on a description of Aunt Tilly's teacup. Is your image precise and meaningful? For example, do you describe the delicate pattern of forget-me-nots that decorates the sides of the fragile cup? And does this description say anything special about Aunt Tilly (perhaps that there's a part of her heart that's delicate and breakable, too)?

> "The thing I have learned through the years is that one idea 'doth' not a novel make. A novel must be several seemingly unrelated ideas that somehow magically come together to create the fabric of the story."
>
> Katherine Paterson

Proofread from Start to Finish

Even readers with the best intentions get turned off by having to muddle through lots of typos or spelling errors, so make sure your writing is as clean as possible. Polishing your writing means proofreading each line, each word, in search of errors.

If you write on a computer, be sure to use the spellchecker. Even if you've spell-checked, read through your work carefully. Maybe catching typos and other mistakes isn't your specialty, so ask a friend or some other person you trust to proofread for you. Offer to do something in exchange for this help.

You may prefer to proofread your work from start to finish, carefully scrutinizing each word. On the other hand, you may favor reading your work several times, looking for different types of errors each time (this is called *pyramid proofing*). To do this, first read over your writing to hear how the whole piece sounds. Then look at each paragraph, stanza, or portion of dialogue separately.

Read each sentence or line, observing how the words hold together. Do you need to be more clear or precise? Finally, look at your word choices: are you repeating yourself or using passive verbs? Don't forget to look at your punctuation, too!

 WRITER'S CORNER

The Elements of Style by William Strunk Jr. and E. B. White (Boston: Allyn & Bacon, 1999). Originally published in 1959, this book has been revised and updated and is considered to be an essential tool for writers and editors. Learn the basic principles of composition, grammar, word usage and misusage, and writing style from this compact, but helpful, book.

21st Century Grammar Book edited by The Princeton Language Institute (New York: Dell Books, 1993). This user-friendly guide to English offers answers to questions about grammar, punctuation, and preferred usage.

Guide to Grammar and Writing
Sponsored by Capital Community-Technical College, Hartford, CT
http://webster.commnet.edu/HP/pages/darling/grammar.htm
This Web page offers accessible information on all aspects of grammar. Some say this is the best one-stop grammar information station online.

Save Original Drafts

In *Bird by Bird: Some Instructions on Writing and Life,* author Anne Lamott talks about how she lives in mortal dread that someone might see her first drafts and be appalled at how truly terrible they are. Many writers live with this fear, and maybe you do, too. Writing is a risk, but it's one you've decided to take. Until your writing is absolutely, positively as good as it gets, don't throw away your original drafts. Save them—even if you think they're horrible, even if you have to hide them where no one will ever think to look.

There's another risk you should know about: revising the life out of your writing. Just about every writer has experienced this at one time or another. You write something and feel pretty inspired, but then you begin to revise—and you revise and revise and revise. Eventually, you may end up with something

> "No passion in the world is equal to the passion to alter someone else's draft."
>
> H. G. Wells

very polished but dull, empty of the raw energy and excitement it once held.

At moments like this, you'll be glad you've saved your drafts. If you've revised something and left it gasping for air, you can dig up the earlier drafts in search of your original inspiration and meaning. Then you can start again.

Another reason to save your first drafts is that you could have cut something—a character, a scene, a passage, a line— that may jump-start a future piece of writing. Sometimes you may even find that certain images from one piece of writing (a poem, perhaps) actually belong in another (such as a short story you're working on). Be on the lookout for writing that wants to get close to other writing.

Did You Know?

 WRITER'S CORNER

Bird by Bird: Some Instructions on Writing and Life by Anne Lamott (New York: Pantheon, 1994). This funny and accessible book covers all kinds of ways to get started and keep going in your writing.

The Observation Deck: A Tool Kit for Writers by Naomi Epel (San Francisco: Chronicle Books, 1998). This book is accompanied by fifty cards containing meditations on writing and tips to spark ideas and help writers through every stage of the creative process.

A Piece of Work: Five Writers Discuss Their Revisions edited by Jay Woodruff (Iowa City, IA: University of Iowa Press, 1993). Five writers describe their revision process and offer examples from their early drafts.

Revision: A Creative Approach to Writing and Rewriting Fiction by David Michael Kaplan (Cincinnati, OH: Story Press, 1997). This book takes you through every stage of the writing process and provides strategies to help pinpoint problems and fix them. The author provides examples from his own work to demonstrate how to revise.

Through rewriting and revising, you learn a great deal about the craft of writing. This is because when you put together a first draft, your main concern is getting your ideas on paper. You don't necessarily pay attention to choosing your best words and images, weaving your plot, finding your rhythm, and fully developing your characters. The process of revising, on the other hand, makes you think about the best way to let your words speak for you. You discover your own voice. You learn to play with language. In the process, you strengthen your skills as a writer.

Revision is a great teacher. In some ways, it teaches you more about writing than *writing* does!

"The wastepaper basket is the writer's best friend."

Isaac Bashevis Singer

CHAPTER 7

Jump-starting Your Writing

I once had a car I named Vampire because it constantly needed to be jump-started. Whenever it refused to start, I'd have to hook up jumper cables to the battery of another car and "steal some juice" to ignite my engine.

Sometimes your writing stalls out. And sometimes, to get going again, you need to steal some juice from another power source.

This chapter shows you ways to reignite your writing, to give it the push it needs to go further. You can use these ideas in the build-it-up or knock-it-down stages (see Chapter 6 for more about that) or whenever you want to add a little spark to your writing.

> "Sometimes the simplest words are the most beautiful. And the most effective."
>
> Robert Cormier

Seek Out New Words

Sometimes seeking new words will lead you in new directions. You can find the words anywhere—a phone book, a dictionary, a magazine, an almanac, a poetry anthology, or a thesaurus. For example, get the Yellow Pages and randomly choose a page; then close your eyes and point to something on it. Now find a creative way to use the word or phrase you pointed to. See what happens.

From a first draft:

> She didn't understand why the car died that day,
> and why her father yelled at her that day, and why
> the sun didn't shine that day, and, most of all,
> why HE, the man of her dreams, didn't bother to
> call that day, the very day he said he would. She
> didn't understand, so she sat on her bed with her
> back against the wall and did nothing.
>
> Genevieve, 17

From the second draft, after taking the words "floor" and "polish" from the Yellow Pages:

> She didn't understand why the car died that day,
> and why her father yelled at her that day, and why
> the sun didn't shine that day, and most of all,
> why HE, the man of her dreams, didn't bother to
> call that day, the very day he said he would.
>
> She didn't understand, so she locked herself
> in her room and sat on the floor, on that strange
> turquoise carpet she never really liked, and
> started polishing her nails. Every so often she
> looked at the phone and felt like she was going
> to cry. "I need to do SOMETHING!" she thought.
> "But what?"
>
> Genevieve, 17

Another way to find new words is to play around with the language of your writing. Take a piece of writing you've done and circle all the nouns (people, places, or things). Or circle all the verbs (action words). Replace whatever words you circled with their opposites.

It doesn't matter whether you come up with the true opposite—just use whatever word pops immediately into your head. What do you do with all these opposite words? You can use some or all of them to freshen up your writing or change it altogether. Think of this exercise as showing the shadow behind your writing.

Before:

> Rain stains the horizon, mist fills the field with blue shade. Five large crows wait atop the cedar tree. Everything is silent. Even me, waiting behind the open sky, my face wet and young.
>
> Cara, 16

After:

> Sun stains the sky, rays fill the parking lot with blue brightness. Five large parakeets wait atop the mall. Nothing is silent. Even you, waiting behind the open ground, your face dry and old.
>
> Cara, 16

> "I love writing. I love the swirl and swing of words as they tangle with human emotions."
>
> James A. Michener

In the above example, the writer might choose to use the phrase "dry and old" somewhere else in the piece, setting up a nice contrast with "wet and young." Or she may want to save an image like "sun-stained sky" for another piece of writing. Or she may just decide to keep the original piece intact. The idea is to think in new directions, get creative, and play with your words.

Change the Setting

Sometimes simply changing the setting of your poem, story, or play can charge the whole piece of writing with electrifying energy.

Suppose you have a poem about walking on the beach. You describe the sand, the waves, the imprint of waves on sand, the hot sun beating down on you as you walk, and your dog trailing behind you. Maybe this poem feels too typical or clichéd. But what if you were to change the setting to the middle of the Great Plains? You may be inspired by images of sand-colored grass waving in the wind, the hot sun beating down on your straw hat, your dog lost in the tall grass. Now you might be ready to create a whole different poem.

Or let's say you've written a murder mystery that takes place in a dark alley at midnight. If you were to change the setting to a shopping mall on a rainy afternoon in the middle of a local high school band competition, you'd have a mystery set in a fresh and unexpected place. Suddenly, your mystery might seem all the more intriguing.

You can also change the time period during which your writing takes place. What if your story was set in the Ice Age, in ancient Egypt, or on the planet Pluto in the year 2050?

Genevieve's writing sample, in a different time period:

> She didn't understand why the horse died that day,
> and why her father, the duke, yelled at her that
> day, and why the sun didn't shine over the castle
> walls that day, and, most of all, why HE, the man
> of her dreams, didn't ride across the drawbridge to
> visit her the very day he said he would. She didn't
> understand, so she sat with her ladies-in-waiting
> on the beautiful furniture and did nothing.
>
> Genevieve, 17

"I make up the characters in my books, but of course my consciousness is filled with every child I've ever known, including my two grand-children, my own kids (I had four) and especially myself as a child, because that person still lives inside me, too."

Lois Lowry

Add a New Character

There's nothing like a new character to breathe life into a dragging story or play: Just pour in one cup of "human-helper," add some spice, and stir. Voilà! You have a whole new dish.

Choose someone who might spark some action in your writing. Maybe this person is funny or entertaining or makes witty remarks. Or perhaps the character is a complaining, mean-spirited person who makes life hard for everyone else in the story. Then again, maybe you create a young girl who keeps hiding essential items (textbooks, wallets, toothbrushes) that belong to the other characters.

You can even let this character narrate some or all of the story. Imagine a stranger wandering into the writing, explaining what's going on, adding a little surprise here and there, and telling you what happens next. This can really liven things up!

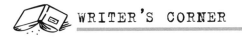 WRITER'S CORNER

Thinking Like a Writer by Lou Willett Stanek (New York: Random House, 1994). This book discusses many aspects of writing, including keeping a journal, using vivid descriptions, and creating memorable characters.

Change the Speaker

You can only see as much in your writing as your speaker sees—that is, the person who's telling the poem, narrating the story, or filling a character's shoes in a play. In a sense, the speaker is like the person behind a window watching the story, poem, play, or essay take place. Windows, with the right angle and light, also *reflect* who's looking through them. And so you come to know the speaker as the piece of writing unfolds.

Using *first-person* point of view means you're writing from the perspective of *I.* The beauty of writing from first person is that you can write directly and clearly from your own experience. And if you're writing fiction, you can write directly and clearly from your main character's or narrator's experience.

You can add a twist to the first-person point of view by characterizing your narrator. Have you ever read *The Great Gatsby* by F. Scott Fitzgerald? He wrote this book in first person, from the viewpoint of the narrator Nick, who plays only a minor role in the story. By using the first person and a narrator who's just on the edge of the story's action, Fitzgerald accomplished two things: (1) he told the story from a semi-objective viewpoint and (2) he had his narrator comment on and evaluate the story as the action occurred. Because Nick is a good guy (not a villain), he's considered a reliable narrator: you believe what he says.

On the other hand, you might read a story where the narrator is "lying" to you (what the narrator says turns out not to be true). For instance, in her novel *Surfacing*, Margaret Atwood created a smart, sensitive, and ultimately untruthful narrator who, it is revealed, is lying to herself. This unreliable narrator tells the story of both the lie and the truth, and why the lie evolved in the first place. In the process, she shares many stories at once.

How can you use these techniques in your own writing? Say you have a story about a couple fighting in a bowling alley. Maybe you told the story in first person, using the man's or the woman's perspective, keeping in mind that either one would be likely to have a biased point of view ("He started it," for example). But perhaps your story feels flat, and you want to liven it up. If so, you could rewrite the story from another character's perspective, such as the shoe-rental guy who overhears the argument. Suppose the woman gave him a hard time when he handed her a pair of bowling shoes, and as a result, he sides with the man she's arguing with. In this case, the new narrator may not be 100 percent reliable, adding a new dimension to the story.

Second-person point of view, in contrast, uses *you* as the main pronoun, allowing you to speak to your reader directly. It's a way of pulling your reader into your writing. If you want your reader to understand *exactly* what it's like to visit your neighbors' house on Thanksgiving, you could write: "You enter the dim house and hear sumo wrestling blasting on the TV. A burnt turkey the size of a peacock sits in the middle of the table. Even the Jell-O looks scary, like it was left over from the meal they served you last year." Your reader feels immediately, if painfully, what this dinner is going to be like.

> "If the story works, that means the characters work. And that's the important element, of course. Your story isn't going to work unless the characters are real and you bring everything to a climax."
>
> Robert Cormier

Sometimes it helps to rewrite something in second person. Let the "speaker" (you, the writer) address the reader directly, even intimately, as if the reader is a good friend listening to the story. See if this point of view helps perk up writing that feels lifeless.

When you write from first or second person, you're focused on one speaker, as opposed to many. On the other hand, writing from the *third-person* point of view (also known as the *omniscient narrator*) gives you tremendous freedom. You get to be every character at once, and you can describe anyone and anything from the viewpoint of a great, all-knowing narrator looking down into the story.

Imagine that you want to describe what Leon the hat salesman looks like. If you're writing in first person and Leon is doing all the talking, you have to find a way to trick him into describing himself. It probably won't ring true to have Leon say, "I'm a tall, middle-aged man in a pinstripe suit with a dyed-blue carnation in my lapel pocket." Instead, he'll have to tell you about himself in bits: "I need to go to the cleaners to get my gray suit, so I can get out of this pinstripe one that doesn't fit me as well."

Using third person, you can describe Leon's suit in detail, without your readers thinking it's strange that one character is so involved in his own clothing. For example, "Leon knew he was getting a little heavy around his middle, but he wished he didn't have to be reminded of it every single time he sat down. While seated, he could feel his gut hanging over his belt like a deflated tire. His tucked-in dress shirt felt itchy and tight. He hated this pinstripe suit, but at least the sport coat hid his bulging stomach."

Sometimes you may feel too confined by writing in first person, and this is where rewriting in third person comes in. Casting the story in *he* or *she* gives you some distance from your writing. This can be especially helpful when you're writing about a painful event or describing a personal incident in your life.

Did You Know?

In 1990, Oscar Hijuelos, author of *The Mambo Kings Play Songs of Love*, was the first Hispanic writer to win a Pulitzer Prize for fiction.

Write Now...

Take a story or poem you wrote in second or third person and rewrite it in first person, from the perspective of a character who isn't directly involved in the main conflict of the story. Does this outsider-looking-in perspective add something new to your writing? You might also try narrating the story from the first-person point of view of the main character. What changes?

Next, take something you originally wrote in first or second person and change it to third person. What can you say now that you couldn't say before? And what can't you say so clearly anymore? See if taking a new approach redirects your writing.

Referring to himself in third person helped the writer of this poem tackle a difficult subject:

```
He wants to do better.
He wants to bring home the right report card,
the right chocolate ice cream,
the right smile on his face.
He wants to walk into the house
and not think that now the yelling will start.
He wants to talk about new cars, sleeping late,
a girl he likes, even what life was like
for his dad a long time ago.
He wants to do better
but every time he walks into the house
his dad tells him something he did
is wrong.
Every time it happens,
he thinks he can't do better.
                                    Stu, 15
```

Speak with Many Voices

Telling a story from the viewpoint of several different characters allows you to let all of them have their say. Many contemporary writers have used this technique of *multiple narrators,*
including Louise Erdrich, Michael Dorris, and Amy Tan. You
can use it, too.

A strong example of multiple narration is Michael Dorris's
novel *A Yellow Raft in Blue Water* The book has three sections,
each of which is narrated in first person by one of three gener-
ations of Native American women.

In the first section, a teen girl named Rayona tells her story
in such a convincing way that the reader gets angry at the people
Rayona's angry with (her mom Christine, and her grandma
Ida). The second section is told from Christine's point of view,
giving the reader a whole new perspective on both Christine's
and Rayona's lives. Because Christine is so resentful of her
mother (Ida), the reader is, too. But by the time Ida gets to tell
her side of the story, the reader comes to understand and even
like her. Each character weaves a strand of the same story, kind
of like a braid, which is why the author starts and ends the book
with braiding imagery.

Did You Know?

Jean-Paul Sartre rejected
the 1964 Nobel Prize in
literature, explaining that
to accept such an award
would compromise his
integrity as a writer.

Write Now...

Let two or three main characters in a story or another piece of
writing tell their side of things. Give them free rein and see
where they go. This is especially helpful when you reread your
writing and find that some of your characters aren't as believable as others. Maybe they aren't as fully developed, which is
why giving them a chance to speak on their own, saying whatever it is they need to say, can lead you in new directions.
Explore what each character cares about, dreams about, lies
about. Do these new insights help you see where to cut, where
to add, where to go?

Jon's side of it:

What really happened was this: Mr. Evans's big dog
got loose and tore up the flower beds in Mrs.
Hill's garden. She got out a rake and went after
the dog, and Mr. Evans got a shovel out and went
after her. These old people ran a lot faster than
I thought they could, and then they caught up to
each other and looked like they were going to
dance instead of fight. Mrs. Hill fell over, but
she got up and started trying to hit Mr. Evans
with her rake. He grabbed a shovel, and they had
what looked like a sword fight with a rake and
shovel. The police had to come and break it up.

Jon, 15

Mrs. Hill's side of it:

I was just sitting on my porch, petting my cat
when that dog came. Now that dog has pulled apart
many of my flowers before, so I picked up the
rake and waved it at him. I wasn't going to hurt
him—I just wanted to scare him. Well, I must have
lost my balance because I fell. When I rolled over
and started to get up, there was Mr. Evans, and he
was waving a shovel at me and calling me a silly
old woman. Mr. Evans has always been so jealous of
my beautiful flowers that I wasn't surprised he
was so mean to me. He started to swing his shovel
at me, so I grabbed my rake and used it to keep
him at bay.

Jon, 15

Mr. Evans's side of it:

Whatever anyone else tells you is a lie. What really happened is that I was carefully weeding my garden when that woman threw herself in the middle of it. And instead of trying to get up, she started pulling out my flowers. I got my shovel so I could replant them right away; it is summer, you know, and those flowers need to be in the ground. This silly woman stood up and started to charge me with her rake. She was yelling that I was old and stupid, and I told her, very politely I might add, that she was old, too. I tried to get away, but she was faster than me. Thank heavens you police officers came and saved my life!

Jon, 15

> "How do you write vital, meaningful dialogue that deepens character-ization, furthers the plot, expands the theme, and sounds real? Let your characters do the talking."
>
> Eve Bunting

Let a Nonhuman Do the Talking

Another way of telling a story is by letting a nonhuman (an animal or object, for example) narrate it. Suppose Fido the dog, or a bowl of chocolate pudding, or a giant turnip from the garden tells the story. Of course, you'd have to pretend this nonhuman has the gift of speech and that others are actually willing to listen to what it has to say. Imagine letting the turnip talk:

Here I am, plucked from my garden and tossed on a hard kitchen counter to await my fate. "Fry it," yells the tall one in the chef's hat. "No, slice it up and throw it in the soup," shouts another. All I can do is wait, knowing that no matter what they decide, my life as turnip has come to a bitter end.

Okay, so maybe turnips don't have anything profound to say, but the point of the exercise is to make your reader feel a little sympathy for the nonhuman character, to care about what happens to it, to see life from its point of view.

Imagine the tales a couch in the teacher's lounge at school might tell. Write a story from the perspective of the baseball you throw around at practice, your pet, the car you drive, the remote control for the TV, or any other object in your life. Another option is to take an existing piece of writing and turn the narrator into a nonhuman. Now this changes everything!

Write Outside the Frame

Everything you write is bound in a frame—not a little gold picture frame that sits on your desk but an imaginary one that holds your writing together. You can write only so much in any given piece. You have certain scenes, characters, and images that all work together to frame your writing. What's *not* included doesn't fit into the frame.

You might, for instance, write a story about a baseball player at the turn of the century who's suddenly transported (complete with his uniform and bat) to present-day New York City. The circumstances of this character's life then and now frame your story in a certain way. For example, you might have a scene about his first time riding the subway or seeing Yankee Stadium. On the other hand, you'd probably leave out a long lecture on how electric cars work. This lesson, while interesting, probably doesn't fit into the frame of your story.

When revising a piece of writing, however, no matter what the form (play, story, poem), you have the opportunity to write *outside* the frame. Many fiction writers, for example, write pages and pages of "back story," that is, descriptions of characters, settings, plot details, and so on that never make it into the actual story. By writing outside the frame, these writers explore their characters, settings, and plot developments on a deeper level. And the more a writer knows about a certain character's motivations, background, and emotions, the easier it is to convey this to the reader.

If you're feeling a bit stuck, as if you don't know where to go in a rewrite, start writing a page or so about what happens

Did You Know?

In 1993, Rita Dove was appointed to a two-year term as Poet Laureate of the United States and Consultant in Poetry to the Library of Congress. She was the youngest person and the first African-American to receive this highest official honor in American letters.

right after your story ends or before it begins (think of this as *before-and-after writing*). Now go back to your original draft and figure out if you started and ended your story, play, or poem in the best possible way. Is there something important you left out? Is there a phrase, scene, or line of dialogue that you may want to use from your before-and-after writing?

Writing outside the frame mainly entails looking just beyond the edge of what you're saying to see what else could be said, what else could be shown. When you're done, your writing might have a new and different frame—a frame that surrounds a more colorful and textured piece of writing.

 WRITER'S CORNER

What's Your Story? A Young Person's Guide to Writing Fiction by Marion Dane Bauer (New York: Clarion Books, 1992). This book discusses how to write fiction, exploring such aspects as character, plot, point of view, dialogue, endings, and revising.

Writing Down the Bones: Freeing the Writer Within by Natalie Goldberg (Boston: Shambhala, 1998). This fun, very readable book is based on Goldberg's Zen master's premise that "If you go deep enough in writing, it will take you everyplace." This book offers dozens of tested ideas, suggestions, and exercises that help new writers get started and seasoned writers keep going.

CHAPTER 8

Going Deeper

Revision lets you dive deeper into your writing and carry more treasures to the surface. If you look, you may find richer, clearer, more authentic writing beneath what's currently on your page. When you strive to bring your work to its fullest potential, you learn what it means to be a writer—and why writing, as challenging as it may be, makes you feel so alive.

Peel Away the Layers

More than anything else, my experience revising my own writing and helping other people revise their writing comes down to this: peel off a layer to get to the next one. In other words, find the poem inside the poem, the story behind the story, the play beyond the play, the essay beneath the essay.

If you view your writing as layers upon layers, you soon realize that the first layer, the one sitting right there on top, is the "easy" one—the one that you produced first because that's what you had the energy, courage, and vision to write at the time. But if you put this writing away and come back to it later to revise, you may see that just below the surface is an idea far more meaningful, accurate, and perhaps even brilliant.

Your writing is like an onion—you have to peel off the papery brown layer to find the first layer of onion. And then you have to peel another layer to reach the stronger part of the onion, the part you really want to use. As you know, peeling the

> "One of the joys of writing: you constantly encounter new experiences."
>
> Philip Pullman

layers this way can sting; sometimes it even brings tears to your eyes. The same goes for your writing. Sometimes it hurts a little, or a lot, to get to the heart of what you're really trying to convey.

I like to think of this process as opening up Russian nesting dolls: you have to keep unscrewing them and looking inside to find the center where one tiny, solid doll hides. In your writing, aim for the center where there's nothing left to open, nothing left to hide.

Go deeper. Dive all the way down. Find the onion of truth, the center solid doll, the treasure at the bottom of the sea. Bring your discoveries to the surface of the page.

Top layer:

My sister is driving me crazy. She comes into my room without knocking, asks me lots of questions, wants to borrow my clothes and earrings, and wants me to take her somewhere (she can't drive yet). I try my best, but last night, I just lost it, and I told her, "Get a life already! Leave me alone." She started crying and ran to her room and locked the door. I felt terrible.

Mimi, 17

Going deeper:

Yes, my sister drives me crazy, but I think some of it is because my parents are getting divorced. My dad just sees us on weekends, and during the week, my mom is very quiet. She won't talk to me about what's really going on, even though I'm seventeen already. I asked her to talk, but she said she didn't want to upset me. I mean, it would be much better if she just told me! I can sense

that she's upset and all, and it makes it worse
when she tries to hide it.
   My sister is pretty upset, too. First she asked
me when our parents would get back together, but
she finally figured that one out. Now she wants me
to be her missing parent—she wants me to be Mom
when we're with Dad, and Dad when we're with Mom.
I can't take this! It's hard enough to watch this
happening, but what makes it worse is that I have
to try not to upset my mom or sister more.
Sometimes I just lose it.

                                          Mimi, 17

Remove the Scaffolding

When you're painting a tall house or building, you usually have to put up scaffolding—a high platform to sit or stand on—so you can get to all the places that are normally out of reach. Sometimes writing is like putting up so much scaffolding: you have to write a whole lot of material to get to what you're *really* trying to reach.

For example, you may start writing about what it's like to fight the crowds at the mall during the holiday season. Maybe you describe all the usual stuff—hordes of people, bright lights, music piped in over the drone of the crowds, lines filled with annoyed customers, and so on. But as you review your work, you notice something happening. You find passages about feeling lost, claustrophobic, alone, and scared, and you wonder what that's all about. Suddenly you remember a time when you were about five and got lost in the mall, and you thought you were going to be lost forever because you couldn't find your way out of the shoe department. All that stuff about holiday crowds was scaffolding—it helped you get at the parts that were out of reach.

Now you can remove the scaffolding.

Recently, I've been through this process myself. While writing a novel about a girl growing up in strange and funny circumstances, I decided that the plot of the novel would revolve around how her house was stolen (not stolen really, but how it got "lost" while being moved from one location to another). The more I wrote, however, the more I realized that the story was really about growing up, and the house had little to do with it. I came to see that I was forcing myself to write the parts about the house. The stolen-house plot was just scaffolding.

But this doesn't mean all my writing was a waste of time and energy. The scaffolding served its purpose: it launched the real story. It helped me say what I really wanted to say.

Let Your Writing Fall in the Swamp

Swamps are mysterious places. They can swallow objects in one place and then shoot them to the surface elsewhere. Branches, dead animals, and missing tennis balls may sink underwater only to emerge miles away. What does this have to do with writing?

Sometimes writing just needs to sink underwater for a while, so it can rise up in a new place. In other words, it needs to fall in the swamp.

If you've been revising a piece of writing over and over again, it's likely that much of the joy and excitement that first propelled the writing is now lost. Perhaps the rewriting process has become a chore, and you're at the point where you can't tell if changing something is good or bad for the writing. If you can't summon any of the enthusiasm you once felt for what you wrote, it's time to give it a rest.

Set up a "swamp file" where your writing can sit and relax for a week, a month, or even longer if necessary. When you're ready to tackle it again, open the file and read what's there. You'll see it in a fresh light.

Did You Know?

Amy Tan, author of *The Joy Luck Club*, published her first story "What the Library Means to Me" when she was eight. Her parents wanted her to be a doctor and a concert pianist on the side, but she defied them and switched her college major to English. Her mother refused to speak to her for six months.

File Away Your "Darlings"

Several years ago, I was at a writer's workshop, sitting on the grass under an overhang halfway up a mountain in New Hampshire. "Kill your darlings," the instructor, poet Jane Kenyon, suddenly announced. "Kill my darlings?" I thought. "You mean, cut my best lines!?" (They're called darlings because they're darling to those of us who wrote them.)

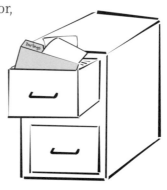

"Yes, precisely," was the answer.

And it was good advice.

Sometimes you write such a great line, paragraph, or passage that you want to keep it in your writing even if it doesn't quite belong there. Even if it slows down your writing. Even if it repeats something you said in a better way elsewhere.

But the line is so good that you don't want to cut it. And you certainly don't want to kill it, right?

So gently remove it and transplant it into your darlings file. This file can be an actual file, a notebook, or even a special drawer. It will be the place to store all the great stuff you edit out of your writing—a place where your darlings are kept safe and sound, so they can bloom into future writings.

I like to keep my darlings file in my bookbag, so I have access to it anytime. This file is the best source for new writing I've ever had. I can open my file, read through my darlings, put one of them at the top of a page . . . and have something to inspire a fresh piece of writing.

Here are some of the things currently residing in my darlings file. If you like any of them, feel free to use them!

- It comes when you're half awake, that sudden knowledge that nothing you know or do has prepared you for your life.

- "Give it up," said the boy in the dream. "Then come running back."

- I'm the girl who dusts the furniture. Sometimes even the corner wall. I try not to dust spiders.

> "I think that one's art is a growth inside one. I do not think one can explain growth. It is silent and subtle. One does not keep digging up a plant to see how it grows."
>
> Emily Carr

130

- So you hold an apricot in your palm—a miniature planet, cool without meaning to be, its pit separated from its pulp by the thinnest hair of space. You hold it and think this will change everything.

- The *dow* in the Dow Jones stock exchange and the Asian *tao* sound exactly the same but are as opposite in meaning as could be.

- Rise blind. Rise alone. Go back to sleep.

Revision is a process in which anything can happen. It can be a launching pad that lifts you off into stories, poems, plays, essays, or other forms of writing that go far beyond anything you ever expected to write.

If you can look beneath the surface of your writing.

If you can cut away what doesn't feed your writing.

If you can let go when you need to let go.

If you can push yourself to keep writing, keep rewriting, keep revising, keep at it.

It's not an easy process, but it's a continual one, for you and for all writers.

You do it so your best writing can surface.

"Read over your compositions and, when you meet a passage which you think is particularly fine, strike it out."

Samuel Johnson

PART 4

Swimming Toward Home: Writing in Community

"Writing can teach us the dignity of speaking the truth, and it spreads out from the page into all of our life, and it should."
Natalie Goldberg

Whatever you write is yours. It belongs to someone else only if you choose to give it to someone else. Your writing is your own as much as your brain, heart, and body are your own. Because your writing belongs to you, it's yours to follow, learn from, and lead.

Throughout this book, you've been learning to write for yourself. You've discovered that writing can be a way to take care of, learn about, protect, push, soothe, and like yourself a little more.

Some of the writing you do is private, just for you, written without the intention of ever showing it to anyone else. But sometimes, you may want to share your writing with others: friends, family, teachers, classmates, your community, the world. You may decide that some of your writing communicates your unique perceptions, perspective, ideas, experiences, and creative gifts.

Sharing your writing is wonderful and scary at the same time. It helps to remember that you're part of a community of writers: writers who have come before you, writers yet to come, and writers all over the world who are experiencing the same challenges as you. Connecting with these writers—and your own readers—can be a source of encouragement, direction, and wisdom. You may feel a new sense of belonging—as if you've come home.

CHAPTER 9

Connecting with Community

Writers often work in isolation, sitting alone at a desk, spilling thoughts and ideas onto paper or a computer keyboard. This can feel very lonely at times. But you're not alone.

As a writer, you're part of a community of writers past, present, and future. Reading the works of other writers can help you appreciate what you've done so far and figure out what you might still want to do. These writers can show you new paths to take in your writing. In short, they can provide encouragement, new ideas, direction, wisdom, and a sense of belonging to a long tradition of words on paper.

But other writers aren't your only source of support. There's also the community in which you live, go to school, work, and hang out. And you can connect with this community through writing classes, readings, and many other avenues.

Whether you choose to go public with your writing or to keep a piece of writing private is completely up to you. Listen to what your heart tells you to do. If, deep down, you feel that something is too private to share, don't give in to pressure from people who ask to read your work or tell you to read it publicly. On the other hand, don't let fears of being told your writing isn't "good enough" stand in your way. If fear is holding you back, show your work to one person you trust to offer you the support and encouragement you need. From there, you can seek out other readers you trust, and perhaps other ways to contribute to your community through your writing.

> "The author is not only himself but his predecessors, and simultaneously he is part of the living tribal fabric, the part that voices what we all know, or should know, and need to hear again."
>
> John Updike

Following are ideas for sharing your writing, connecting with other writers, sending your writing out to the wider world, and much more.

Find a Secret Writing Mentor

Once you begin reading the works of a variety of writers, you may find one who speaks to you above all the rest. Maybe this writer develops characters who remind you of yourself, speaks in a voice you can easily identify with, creates settings that feel comfortable and familiar, or weaves imaginative plots that sweep you away. You can let this writer be your secret writing mentor—someone you turn to for ideas, inspiration, guidance, advice, and help. A mentor is like a teacher, counselor, friend, and confidant all in one package.

Some of my best teachers have been other writers who have never even met me. For many years, I read the work of American poet Adrienne Rich, and in reading all of her poems over and over, aloud sometimes, I found myself learning more about what I wanted to say and how I could say it. Although I've never met Adrienne Rich, she was my secret writing mentor for about eight years. I went on to learn from other secret mentors: writers William Stafford, Annie Dillard, and Toni Morrison. Their words made me feel motivated, challenged, inspired, alive.

If you want a secret writing mentor, choose a writer who really speaks to you; then read all you can by and about that person. You can probably find biographies (maybe even an autobiography) about the writer in your school or local library, or online if you have access to the Internet. Read everything the writer wrote. Look for personal interviews, critical reviews and analyses of his or her work, and anything else that will help you learn more about the writer's life and life's work.

Exploring this secret mentor's career is a great way to see how another writer's body of work grows and changes over time. This will give you insight into how you can approach your own writing and make the most of your creativity.

Did You Know?

Nineteenth-century poet Emily Dickinson preferred to live a life of solitude and was rarely seen by friends and neighbors. She was known in the town of Amherst, Massachusetts, as the legend who dressed in white. Some scholars believe Dickinson purposely chose a life of solitude so she could write, because during this period, it was difficult for women writers to pursue their craft.

After studying the writer's work, you might find yourself wondering how your secret mentor would approach a challenging piece of your writing, come up with a realistic plot, create a believable character, or get a line of dialogue just right. Or perhaps you'll even find yourself wandering down the street chatting (in your head, of course) with Judy Blume, Langston Hughes, Alice Walker, or Gary Paulsen. And why not? As long as you don't talk out loud during this private conversation, people won't stare at you like you're crazy. You can ask your favorite writer whatever you want about his or her writing and life—and about yours. You just may discover the answer you've been searching for.

 Write Now...

Write an imaginary conversation between you and your secret writing mentor (or a writer you admire). What would the two of you talk about if you could meet? Are there any specific questions you'd like to ask about your own writing? What advice might the writer give you—and what advice might you give in return? The conversation can be as long or short as you want. Feel free to revisit your secret writing mentor whenever you need to talk.

```
My dialogue takes place on an airplane where I'm
seated, magically enough, beside Stephen King, my
favorite writer. Of course, we're in first class
(this is fantasy!). I immediately pull out a story
I wrote about a horse who dies and comes back to
haunt a small town. King reads it eagerly, laughing
at all the funny parts and nodding in approval.

SK: This is actually very good.
ME: You're just saying that.
```

SK: No, I mean it. You've developed this horse so well, I feel like I know him. And the plot, well, it just grabbed me. I think you have a real future as a writer.

ME: Oh, you don't have to be so nice.

SK: I'm not being "so nice." Do you know how many people send me stories? I read stories all the time, but yours really has something.

ME: So are you going to publish it?

SK: (laughing) Not so fast, but I'll tell you what I'm going to do: Here's my business card with my email address. Email me your next story, and I'll give you some tips on making it better.

ME: You mean it?

SK: I sure do. As for this story, I think you can make it even better by describing the forest in more detail.

ME: Yeah, I was thinking the same thing. Do you think I should cut the last paragraph?

SK: Yes, I do. The next-to-last paragraph would be a much better ending. Oh, look, it's dinnertime. Let's eat our gourmet airplane food and talk about your story some more.

Carol, 15

Find an Actual Mentor

When I started writing poetry in high school, a few of my teachers showed interest in my work. They took time to read my writing and sent me to the library to read other writers. They encouraged me and gave me hope. Their small kindnesses—such as reading a new poem of mine over lunch in the teacher's lounge—were a huge source of support for me and motivated me to pursue my writing. Without the encouragement of these teachers, I'm not sure I would have kept filling up pages and notebooks with poems. I'm grateful I did, though.

I was lucky: these mentors came to me when I needed them. But you can actively search out potential mentors—people who can offer you knowledge, encouragement, and resources that you might not otherwise find. Is there an adult you know (a teacher, youth group leader, friend's parent, or member of your community) who might be interested in mentoring you? Perhaps a local writer or artist is available to talk or spend time with you. Find someone who's willing to look at your writing occasionally, give you constructive criticism, make suggestions about books or articles to read, and generally offer you support.

Make a list of some potential mentors; then choose one to talk to first. Tell this person that you're interested in writing and are looking for someone to meet with one-on-one for ideas and input. Explain that you'd like some honest feedback on your writing. Find out if the person is willing to be a mentor and whether he or she is available in person, or by phone or email. If this potential mentor doesn't work out, don't feel defeated. Try someone else on your list.

As you work with your mentor, see how the relationship evolves. If the two of you seem to get along well and you're receiving the help you need, that's great. Keep meeting for as long as you both want to.

Here are three tips for getting the most out of the mentor relationship:

1. Remember that your mentor is giving you the gift of personal time. It's appropriate to offer a favor in return every once in a while (treat your mentor to lunch, for example, or send a handmade card). You don't have to do anything fancy or expensive. It's the thought that counts.

2. Come prepared when you meet. Bring writing samples, rewrites you've completed, questions, and topics for discussion. Listen respectfully to any feedback your mentor gives you. You may even want to take notes.

Did You Know?

F. Scott Fitzgerald, author of *The Great Gatsby*, brought a young Ernest Hemingway to the attention of his editor at Scribner's. Hemingway went on to author such novels as *The Old Man and the Sea*, *For Whom the Bell Tolls*, and *The Sun Also Rises*.

3. Follow up. If your mentor has suggested, for example, that you cut a scene from a play you're writing, let him or her know what you ultimately decided to do. Did you cut the scene and realize it was the right decision? Did you shorten the scene so it flowed better? Did you think of a good reason to keep the scene in? Let your mentor know if the feedback you've been given is helpful. If a suggestion your mentor made really inspired you, follow up with a thank-you note or call.

One of the benefits of working with a mentor is that, over time, you'll develop your own inner mentor. As you gain new skills, you'll become a better judge of your writing, of the comments and suggestions you receive, and of ways to revise. And once you've learned to mentor yourself, you can think about whether you'd like to mentor someone else!

Be a Mentor

Suppose you've been writing for a while and you've grown more confident about your skills. Maybe you're ready to return the favor of mentorship by becoming one yourself. Is there a budding writer you know who could use your help? Offering your wisdom to someone who's just starting out is a wonderful way for you to grow as a writer.

If you become a mentor, remember that what a young writer needs more than anything is encouragement. Start off each session by pointing out what's good about the person's writing. Later, you can talk about ways to strengthen the writing, offer a few book suggestions, and even show some examples of your own work and changes you've made to it.

Be sure to avoid the temptation of rewriting the young writer's work. Instead, offer suggestions and comments and let him or her take it from there. Remember, too, that you shouldn't expect the person you're mentoring to heed *every* suggestion you make. All writers need to develop their own sense of judgment, and sometimes they reject good advice along the way. This is part of the learning process, so don't take it personally.

Did You Know?

Louise Erdrich's first novel *Love Medicine* was rejected by several publishing houses. Her late husband, author Michael Dorris, posed as her literary agent and resubmitted the novel, which eventually sold 400,000 copies in hardback and won the 1984 National Book Critics Circle Award.

There's another benefit of mentoring: seeing the excitement and potential of a writer who's just getting started. This can help sustain, or even renew, your own enthusiasm for writing!

Take a Writing Class

A great way to connect with other writers is to take writing classes, sometimes referred to as workshops, seminars, or sessions. You might be able to take a class in creative writing, fiction writing, poetry, or screenwriting at your school. If not, look for classes offered in your community. Colleges and public universities usually offer a variety of courses for anyone interested in writing. You could go to your local library for information on writer's workshops, or you might locate a writing class through a city parks and recreation program or a local arts center or museum. In larger cities, you can often find writing centers that hold regular workshops; a local YMCA/YWCA may also sponsor a writing program.

In a writing class, you'll be encouraged not only to polish your skills as a writer but also to share your work with others in the class. Although you may feel self-conscious at first, it can be rewarding to have other people read what you've written and hear their comments. One of the most inspiring workshops I ever held was an eight-month series of classes involving older women (mostly over age seventy) and "at-risk" teenage girls. The women gave the girls so much encouragement, wisdom, and love; in return, the girls gave the women a sense of enthusiasm and a better idea of what it's like to grow up today. Everyone left the class with stronger writing abilities *and* something more: a clearer picture of who they are and what they want to do with the rest of their lives. It was an experience none of us could soon forget.

> "People are always asking me if writing can be taught. My answer is, 'No—I don't think writing can be taught.' But on the other hand, if I were a young writer and convinced of my talent, I could do a lot worse than to attend a really good college workshop."
>
> Truman Capote

WRITER'S CORNER

Inkspot: The Writer's Resource

http://www.inkspot.com

Inkspot offers helpful information about the writers' market, writing tips, articles and interviews with professional authors and editors, and links to several other writing resources available on the Internet. It also includes a special "For Young Writers" section.

Pacific News YO (Youth Outlook)

660 Market Street, Room 210

San Francisco, CA 94104

(415) 438-4755

http://www.pacificnews.org/yo/

This is a monthly newspaper by and about young people, with content ranging from arts and current events to political issues. You can read examples of young people's works on their Web site. Youth Outlook is also available in hard copy by subscription.

Talk City's The InSite

http://www.talkcity.com/theinsite

The InSite, created to help teens connect with other teens who want to make this planet a cleaner, safer, and more equitable place, has a gallery where you can submit stories, poems, reviews, art, photography, and music. It also offers opportunities for teens and young adults who are interested in writing, reporting, and editing for the site.

Teen Link

http://www.nypl.org/branch/teen/teenlink.html

The New York Public Library has created a page that features homework help, information about college and careers, compilations of booklists, and an anthology of teen writing. Read the writings of other teens and submit your own work.

The Young Writers Club

http://www.cs.bilkent.edu.tr/~david/derya/ywc.html

The Young Writers Club aims to encourage kids of all ages to enjoy writing as a creative pastime by getting them to share their work and help each other improve their writing abilities. The site includes book and film reviews, StoryBooks where you can help decide what happens next in the story, ideas for research projects, the Word of the Week to help improve your vocabulary, and a list of online writing-related clubs and resources.

Give a Reading

One of the best ways to encourage yourself as a writer is to share your writing with an audience at a public reading. It may feel scary to get up on stage, but it can also be very rewarding.

A young writer once said to me, "I keep telling myself 'Put yourself at risk.'" She had to push herself a little and take chances she might normally shy away from. But once she began reading her poems at a local coffeehouse, she found ways to revise and improve her work. Reading aloud and getting the immediate feedback of a live audience helped her strengthen her poems *and* her confidence as a writer.

I've found that when I give readings, I can almost feel the presence of people listening. I can sense the energy and excitement of the audience coming through me as I read. If you think you might want to experience what it's like to give a reading, check out the resources your school or community has to offer. Is there an open-microphone night where you can read your fiction or poetry aloud? Are there any local coffeehouses where you might perform a reading? How about a book-store? Or maybe your place of worship (if you have one)? Are there other places where writers can gather and show their work?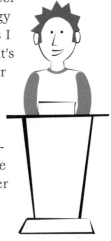

If you have few resources at school or in your com-munity, how about organizing your own reading? Are there other students you know who are interested in writing and could join you in your efforts? Talk to your teach-ers or other school personnel about using a stage to hold the reading.

Once you've found a comfortable location, ask four or more people to read for five to ten minutes each (if you'd like, you can have a timekeeper who signals people if they go on for too long). Advertise your reading around school by hanging posters or handing out flyers. It's a nice touch to provide cookies and punch at the end of the reading, so people feel like they're at a reception and have the opportunity to tell the writers how much they enjoyed the reading. You may have to get special permission to bring food and drinks, though.

As far as preparing yourself to read aloud, the key is *practice*. I get ready by standing on a chair in the basement, reading my work out loud to an imaginary audience. Why a chair? Who knows . . . it makes me feel important, I guess. You can stand in front of a mirror, read to a parent or friend, or even try a practice session on the stage you'll actually perform on—whatever works for you. Practicing over and over will help you get more comfortable reading aloud, so you're not as likely to stumble over the words when you read in front of a group.

When you perform for a live audience, keep the following tips in mind:

1. Read slowly. Most of us read our stuff too fast when there's an audience involved. Maybe we're afraid of boring people or taking too much of their time. Or maybe nervousness makes us try to rush to get it over with. But the truth is, the audience is there to hear a live performance, and everyone will feel more satisfied listening to a writer who reads clearly, rather than one who mumbles the words at top speed.

2. Read loudly. You'll need to intentionally read louder than you're used to. Project your voice so that it reaches everyone, especially the people sitting way in the back of the room. If possible, practice using a microphone beforehand, so you're comfortable with it. If you can't do that, rehearse in front of a friend who's sitting at the back of the room. Get comfortable with the volume you'll use at the actual reading.

3. Read only for the allotted time period. If you're supposed to read for five minutes, don't read for twenty. Choose a short piece. It's not fair to the audience or the other readers when one person hogs the spotlight.

4. Don't apologize or express your doubts aloud. If you're nervous, you might say things like, "This isn't as good as anyone else's" or "I'm sorry I'm making you listen to this." These put-downs make other people uncomfortable, and it's never helpful to say bad things about yourself in public. Be brave. Act confident, so you *feel* confident.

5. Accept praise. It's normal to feel a little awkward when people clap for you or say nice things about your work. You may feel self-conscious, as if you're smiling too much or looking conceited in front of other people. But you deserve any praise that comes your way! After all, you've worked hard and you've dared to share your work with an audience. Listen to the applause and compliments. If people say they enjoyed your reading, say, "Thank you. I'm glad you could come."

Start a Writing Group

You can form your own writer's group with friends and other people you know who like to write. This is a great way to practice your skills, get ideas and feedback from other writers, and become more comfortable expressing yourself in a group. Your writing group can do writing exercises from this book, from other writing guides, or even ones you make up yourselves. You can read your work aloud during each meeting or have everyone bring photocopies of their work for other people to write their responses on. Take turns offering comments, critiquing one another's work, and discussing ways to revise.

You may want to set a few ground rules for the group ahead of time. For example, you might decide to gather at the same place each time or take turns hosting the meetings. Make sure everyone really listens when someone gives a reading—no talking, reading other materials, or doodling. Thank each writer for sharing his or her work, so everyone feels welcome and appreciated.

As you critique each other's work, keep in mind how it feels to hear other people's comments. Treat others as *you* want to be treated. Sharing work is tough to do, and it's important to show one another compassion (yet be honest, too).

Always focus your comments on what *works* in the writing and suggest ways to make the writing stronger, instead of pointing out flaws. In other words, be *positive*. You can comment on images, character development, setting, plot, rhythm, or even how the writing moved you. The best question to keep in mind is "What can the writer do to bring more life to the surface of

Did You Know?

Sandra Benítez spent three years working on her first novel (a mystery) only to have it heavily criticized at a writer's conference. She had written it under her maiden name, Sandy Ables. Success came after she changed Sandy to Sandra, adopted her mother's Puerto Rican surname, and began to write about what was important to her—her Latin-American roots. Her first published novel *A Place Where the Sea Remembers* earned her comparisons to the work of famous writers like Laura Esquivel and Sandra Cisneros.

this writing?" And remember that you're critiquing the writing, not the writer. Keep your comments focused on the work itself.

When *your* work is being critiqued, remember not to take any comments too personally. Listen carefully and take notes about what other people have to say. Don't feel like you have to defend yourself or your work—this only gets in the way and creates hard feelings. Later, when you're back home and ready to revise your writing, you can review the comments and decide what's best for your writing.

Try to Get Published

Does your school have a publication of students' creative writing? If so, get involved. Find out if you can contribute your work or help put together the publication. Meeting with other students who enjoy writing can help you feel connected to a writing community.

If you want to publish your work in some other forum, consider viewing some writing sites online, checking out teen magazines that feature young writers, or going to the library to research contests you can enter or publishers you can send your work to. See the "Writer's Corner" on pages 146–147 for a list of resources you might be interested in.

If you decide to send your work to a contest or a publisher, make sure you request a set of guidelines telling you exactly what to do. Just about every contest or publication has a set of printed guidelines for writers who want to submit their work. For example, there may be a contest fee you have to send, which is used to help pay the judges reviewing your submission. Or, if you're submitting a longer work like a novel, you usually don't have to send the whole book; instead, you submit an outline of the book and a sample chapter.

A few warnings: Some publishers charge a *reading fee* to review your manuscript (this is different than a contest fee), and you may want to avoid such publishers. The fees can be high and may even be a way to cheat writers. Also, think twice if a publisher tells you that your poem or story will be published in an anthology if you agree to purchase it. The cost of these

Did You Know?

James A. Michener didn't publish his first novel, *Tales of the South Pacific,* until he was forty-one, but it earned him the 1948 Pulitzer Prize and was adapted into the famous musical *South Pacific.*

anthologies can be very high (as much as $50 or $100). Similarly, if a publisher offers to print your book for several hundred—or thousand—dollars, keep in mind that such "vanity presses" usually don't distribute the books they print to stores or through catalogs. So you end up selling the book yourself after assuming the cost of printing it. (Tip: If you want to publish your work for friends and family, do it yourself using a computer. Create a "limited edition" complete with a handmade cover.)

If you're sending your work to a magazine, book publisher, contest, or other source, always include a *query letter* that describes your submission, your writing background, and your reasons for choosing this publisher. Be neat and professional: never submit a handwritten piece. If you don't have access to a computer, type your work. Make sure you've proofread it, so it's clean and easy to read. Always send a photocopy—*never* an original—because you never know when your work might get lost in the mail or in the shuffle of other submissions that publishers receive every day. Be sure to include a self-addressed, stamped envelope with your work, so it can be returned to you if it isn't published.

Be aware that getting published takes time. As a poet, I typically send out a dozen packets, containing about six poems each, to various literary magazines. Within six months, eleven out of the twelve packets usually come back with little rejection slips in them, saying something like "Sorry, this doesn't meet the needs of our publication at this time." But I don't get too discouraged because, if I'm lucky, some of the slips have handwritten notes from editors with comments like "Interesting, send us more." Then I follow up by sending several more poems to these editors.

Stuart Murdoch
144 Broadway
New York, NY 10011

The one packet that *didn't* get sent back to me is usually returned about six months later with a letter saying that one of my poems will be published. This is always exciting no matter how many times it happens. Usually, the poem appears in the magazine about a year (and sometimes two years) later. This is the nature of magazine and book publishing—it typically takes a long time before you see your work in print!

Because of all the waiting involved, it's pointless to hang out by your mailbox each day anxiously awaiting some news from a publisher or contest. Note on your calendar when and where you sent your work, and after about two to six months (depending on the publisher's guidelines), check to see whether you've gotten a response. If you haven't, feel free to write or call the publisher to ask about the status of your submission.

 WRITER'S CORNER

The Market Guide for Young Writers: Where and How to Sell What You Write by Kathy Henderson (Cincinnati, OH: Writer's Digest Books, 1996). This book offers tips and suggestions on how to prepare your work for publication and provides a list of contests, magazines, and publishers who accept and encourage submissions from young people.

Poet and Writer
72 Spring Street
New York, NY 10012
(212) 226-3586
This publication has interviews with writers and lots of discussions on what makes writing strong, plus lists of contests and publications. Keep in mind that many of the contests listed are very competitive.

The Writer, Inc.
120 Boylston Street
Boston, MA 02116-4615
1-888-273-8214
http://www.channel1.com/thewriter/
Each month, this magazine provides articles full of writing tips by leading writers and information on how and where to submit manuscripts. Check out their Web site for additional links and resources related to writing and publishing.

The Writer's Market edited by Kirsten Holm (Cincinnati, OH: Writer's Digest Books, 1997). This book has chapters on writing queries and negotiating contracts, plus a comprehensive listing of more than 4,200 book publishers, magazines, greeting-card companies, writing contests, and online markets. Check out the Writer's Digest Web site for lots more resources and information about getting published and connecting with the writing community: *http://www.writersdigest.com.*

Did You Know?

In 1930, Sinclair Lewis was the first U.S. writer to be awarded the Nobel Prize for literature. To date, ten people from the United States have won this honor, including Ernest Hemingway, John Steinbeck, Toni Morrison, and William Faulkner.

The Young Person's Guide to Becoming a Writer: How to Develop Your Talent, Write Like a Pro—and Get Published! by Janet E. Grant (Minneapolis: Free Spirit Publishing, 1995). This guide to beginning and sustaining a writing career includes lots of information on getting started, revising your work, hunting down publishers, preparing manuscripts for submission, and more.

Writes of Passage

P.O. Box 1935
Livingston, NJ 07039
http://www.writes.org/
Writes of Passage is an outlet for teens who have something to say and provides an opportunity for them to showcase their work. It includes lots of great writing tips, poetry, stories, resources, and more written by and for teens.

"For two years I received nothing but rejections."

Judy Blume

If your work is rejected, don't get discouraged and give up writing. *All* writers have to face rejection, and though it may be painful, you can handle it. I know a writer who has saved every rejection slip he's ever gotten, and he plans to wallpaper his bathroom with them one day. For my part, I simply toss my rejection slips in the trash. I try not to take it personally when a publisher decides not to use my work, because there's a good chance it simply didn't fit the publisher's needs—and not necessarily because the editor thought my writing wasn't good enough.

If you want, after a rejection, reread your work and see how it feels now that you've gotten some distance from it. Is it as polished as you'd like? If not, go back and fine-tune it (for ideas on revising, see Part 3). But if you're comfortable with your work as it is, consider submitting it to another publisher. Keep trying.

"I started collecting rejection slips when I was 12."

Stephen King

If your work is accepted, congratulations! Your acceptance letter will probably explain what your next step should be. You may receive payment for a poem that will be published, for example, or you may need to sign a contract. If you have to return a signed form or contract, read it carefully so you know exactly what to expect. If you don't understand something on the form or contract, ask someone for help. Then relax and celebrate!

One thing you may want to know is that a little success can actually make it hard to continue writing. Once you've gotten

"Work inspires inspiration. Keep working. If you succeed, keep working. If you fail, keep working. If you're interested, keep working. If you're bored, keep working."

Michael Crichton

published or received an award, for example, you may feel pressured to create something "as good" as your earlier work. This can lead to what's known as a *success block* where you don't feel creative or inspired anymore. Write anyway. Scribble in your journal, freewrite, or revise some of your old writing. Keep your pen moving, so you never forget that you're a writer.

A Final Word

Writing is a lifetime process. The more you write, the more you come to know your own dreams, fears, thoughts, wishes, and goals for the future. Think of writing as the conduit between what's inside you and what you express to the world.

I still sit on concrete steps and write, just like I did when I was a teenager. I still write in waiting rooms, on long car trips, in cafés, and in my office. For me, writing continues to be a way of understanding the world and how I fit into it.

Your writing can show you, again and again, ways to see, hear, feel, and say more—now and always.

Index

About the Author

Caryn Mirriam-Goldberg decided to be a poet when she was fourteen, but by the time she was eighteen, she thought she had to listen to all those people who said, "A *poet?* You'd better get a *real* job—you can't support yourself as a poet."

She left New Jersey and New York where she grew up and headed to Missouri. There she attended journalism school, became a reporter, and worked for five years as a political organizer. She also fixed roofs, typeset business cards, waited tables, presented workshops on insulating houses, sold ads, wrote marketing copy, put coupons in bags of dog food on an assembly line, cleaned houses, and did many other jobs. But what she really loved was poetry, and eventually, she left those jobs one by one, moved to Kansas, and went back to school, where she had to write to earn her degrees.

Along the way to earning an M.A. and a Ph.D. in English, Caryn realized she wanted to teach writing—to help people of all ages and backgrounds find ways to express what was most meaningful to them. She has taught at the University of Kansas, at Haskell Indian Nations University, and, most recently, at Goddard College in Plainfield, Vermont. She also works as a freelance writer for various organizations, companies, and publishers and leads creative writing workshops for writers of all ages. She still writes poetry, as well as fiction and essays, and her first book of poetry, *Lot's Wife,* was recently published by Woodley Press. She also has published a young-adult biography of author Sandra Cisneros (Enslow Press).

Currently, Caryn lives and writes, with her husband, children, and a houseful of pets, in a big field full of crows and tall grass in eastern Kansas.

Other Great Books from Free Spirit

Totally Private & Personal
Journaling Ideas for Girls
and Young Women
by Jessica Wilber
Written by a fourteen-year-old,
this book offers personal
insights, experiences, and
guidance—journaling tips and
suggestions, advice about being a girl, things
to do, and more. Serious and funny, upbeat
and down-to-earth. For ages 11–16.
$8.95; 168 pp.; softcover; 5⅛" x 7⅜"

Making Every Day Count
Daily Readings for Young People
on Solving Problems, Setting Goals,
& Feeling Good About Yourself
*by Pamela Espeland and
Elizabeth Verdick*
Each entry in this book of daily
readings includes a thought-
provoking quotation, a brief essay, and a
positive "I"-statement that relates the entry
to the reader's own life. For ages 11 & up.
$9.95; 392 pp.; softcover; 4¼" x 6¼"

The Young Person's Guide to Becoming a Writer
How to Develop Your Talent, Write
Like a Pro—and Get Published!
by Janet E. Grant
Do you love to write? This
book tells you how to develop
your own writing style, evalu-
ate your work, experiment with genres—and
get published. Includes success stories and tips
from other young writers. For ages 12 & up.
$13.95; 184 pp.; softcover; 6" x 9"

Making the Most of Today
Daily Readings for Young People
on Self-Awareness, Creativity,
& Self-Esteem
*by Pamela Espeland and
Rosemary Wallner*
Quotes from famous figures
guide you through a year of
positive thinking, problem solving, and
practical lifeskills—the keys to making the
most of every day. For ages 11 & up.
$9.95; 392 pp.; softcover; 4¼" x 6¼"

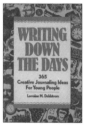

Writing Down the Days
365 Creative Journaling Ideas
For Young People
by Lorraine M. Dahlstrom
A year's worth of fresh, inno-
vative creative writing assign-
ments—some serious, some
silly—all linked to the calendar year. Each assignment
features a person, fact, or event that gives
special meaning to the day. Ideal for classroom,
homeschool, or home. For ages 12 & up.
$12.95; 176 pp.; softcover; illus.; 6" x 9"

What Teens Need to Succeed
Proven, Practical Ways to
Shape Your Own Future
*by Peter L. Benson, Ph.D.,
Judy Galbraith, M.A.,
and Pamela Espeland*
Based on a national survey,
this book describes 40 devel-
opmental "assets" all teens need to succeed in
life, then gives hundreds of suggestions teens
can use to build assets wherever they are.
For ages 11 & up.
$14.95; 368 pp.; softcover; illus.; 7¼" x 9¼"

To place an order or to request a free catalog of SELF–HELP FOR KIDS® *and*
SELF–HELP FOR TEENS® *materials, please write, call, email, or visit our Web site:*

Free Spirit Publishing Inc.
400 First Avenue North • Suite 616 • Minneapolis, MN 55401-1724
toll-free 800.735.7323 • local 612.338.2068 • fax 612.337.5050
help4kids@freespirit.com • www.freespirit.com